What People Are Saying About James W. Goll and *Strike the Mark*

"Prayer changes the conditions upon which the decisions of God are made. When we pray, good things happen. When we don't, the power of darkness has its way. It's a great tragedy to see how many believers look upon what darkness has accomplished and call it the sovereign will of God. According to Scripture, God's will is 'on earth as it is in heaven.' Prayer enables us to partner with Him to make His will/kingdom manifest here in this world. *Strike the Mark* focuses on this very thing. James Goll encourages us all to see intercession as the vehicle God uses to release His glory into every situation. I urge you to read this book and to stand in the place of prayer for your family, city, and nation. Give heaven a target, and watch God's glorious will increasingly manifest on the earth."

—*Bill Johnson*
Bethel Church, Redding, CA
Author, *The Way of Life* and *Raising Giant-Killers*

"Simply stated, I know of no one more qualified to write on prayer than James Goll—*no one!* He lives a supernatural life, undoubtedly because he lives a life of prayer. James may be the most unique blend of scholasticism and prophetic revelation of anyone I know. Regardless of your current understanding of prayer, read *Strike the Mark* and you will become more effective in intercession...guaranteed."

—*Dr. Dutch Sheets*
Dutch Sheets Ministries
Colorado Springs, CO

"James Goll is a longtime friend and a leading voice in the prayer movement around the world. This is a man who knows how to touch heaven, and the results of those prayers are seen and felt. People groups are saved. Gates open. Demons flee. Lives are transformed forever by the presence of God released through a life invested in relationship with the Father. *Strike the Mark* is filled with powerful truths that will enable all who are looking to revolutionize their prayer life to spiral higher."

—*Jane Hansen Hoyt*
CEO/President, Aglow International

"I have known James Goll for nearly forty years and appreciate the unique gifting from the Lord that he carries, especially in the area of intercession and the prophetic. He is one of God's treasures and an apostle of prayer. I am glad that he has been able to share with us from his rich store of revelation in *Strike the Mark: Powerfully Targeted Prayers for Victory and Breakthrough*. This book could not come at a more strategic hour as we see powers of darkness on the rise in our nation and the nations of the world. This present-day tool will open new doors for you to sharpen your prayers and focus your intercession for accuracy and effectiveness. *Strike the Mark* will equip and empower you to stand on the frontlines of battle with confidence."

—*Mahesh and Bonnie Chavda*
Senior Pastors, All Nations Church, Charlotte, NC

"James Goll hits the target once again in his latest intercessory prayer book, *Strike the Mark*. This book is destined to become a classic in the modern-day prayer movement. James's masterful ability to offer Scripture to anchor personal experiences in prayer—along with his ability to inspire faith in our hearts that God will move at the sound of our voice as we persevere—will cause you to rise up and 'strike the ground' until you win every battle you're facing. (See 2 Kings 13:14–19.) This book is a must-read for every prayer warrior."

—*Jennifer LeClaire*
Best-selling author, *Waging Prophetic Warfare*
Senior leader, Awakening House of Prayer movement

"James Goll has been a dear brother and friend for many years. His great passion to connect with the heart of God carries forward through his prophetic voice. Together, we are witnessing God move mightily today through the intercession of generations. Fruits of united intercession lead to revival, and revival is birthed through each of us. *Strike the Mark: Powerfully Targeted Prayers for Victory and Breakthrough* is a resource rich with insights and tools for your personal prayer life. The wisdom found in this book will equip and enable generations to spark Spirit-led movements, inspire kingdom transformation, and unite the family of God for the global revival and reformation emerging today."

—*Dr. Ché Ahn*
President, Harvest International Ministry
Senior Pastor, HRock Church International
Chancellor, Wagner University

"James Goll's book *Strike the Mark* will open up new avenues of prayer to you. It is deeply, spiritually practical! Everyone—from a beginning 'pray-er' to a seasoned intercessor—will find this a resource to heighten their prayer life in a way that produces great results!"

—*Dr. Cindy Jacobs*
Generals International

"*Strike the Mark: Powerfully Targeted Prayers for Victory and Breakthrough* by Dr. James Goll is a perfectly timed work. The greatest prayer movement known to the church is emerging and will usher in a full manifestation of the kingdom in these coming days. Prayer is key! God's agendas only manifest in the earth through the gateway of prayer and intercession. This book is one you should read, apply, and keep in your library for further reference."

—*Dr. Patricia King*
Founder, Patricia King Ministries

"In God's kingdom, breakthrough prayer operates under the law of accumulation. Each time we pray, God gives us more revelation of His Word and purposes, and we pray fresh prayers according to what He reveals to us. In *Strike the Mark*, James Goll unfolds the power of such prayer. He shares deep wisdom and knowledge from decades of interceding and ministering before the Lord. I recommend this important work. Among the many essential topics he covers, James highlights the vital components of persevering in the presence of God and praying from the perspective that Christ has already won the spiritual battle once and for all. He writes, 'From a position of victory, we pray prayers of victory. We proclaim the all-sufficiency of our God and we draw heaven's blessings down to earth.' Only with this perspective can we pray effectively, bringing forth supernatural and eternal results for the kingdom!"

—*Apostle Guillermo Maldonado*
Best-selling author, *Breakthrough Prayer*
King Jesus International Ministry, Miami, FL

"In our conflict-ridden world, prayer is a way bringing God's purposes into manifestation. *Strike the Mark* is a concise, well-written blueprint for sharpening our prayers and making them more effective. James Goll's work is like the voice of a seasoned coach training his team for a championship game. If we will follow his directives, we will win life's most significant contests."

—*Dr. Harry R. Jackson Jr.*
Senior Pastor, Hope Christian Church, Beltsville, MD

"James Goll has become a dear friend of ours in recent years. Among the many things we love about James is how passionate he is about equipping the body of Christ with practical and inspirational tools and how he loves prayer that leads to the presence of God. If you need a manual to help you grow in prayer and intercession, then *Strike the Mark* is written with you in mind. We know firsthand that he is a man of prayer and power, and because of his diligence in his walk with God, he carries authority in these areas."

—*Henry and Alex Seeley*
Cofounders, The Belonging Co, Nashville, TN

"When I first met James Goll, it was at a meeting and he was asked to pray. When he opened his mouth, the anointing came forth in great power. I was immediately impressed with the depth of his anointing in prayer. *Strike the Mark* shows you the depth of anointing James still has for prayer. This book offers simple but profound insights into intercession. You will find many nuggets providing a clearer understanding of prayer and how it works. And you, too, will be able to *Strike the Mark* in your prayer life!"

—*Elizabeth (Beth) Alves*
Increase International
Best-selling author, *Becoming a Prayer Warrior*

"In *Strike the Mark*, James Goll compares prayer to the harmonious music of an orchestra, in which each believer plays an indispensable part. The Scriptures instruct us to pray '*all kinds of prayers*' (Ephesians 6:8 NIV). James urges us to discover our particular 'sound,' or 'instrument,' in prayer; enlarge the scope of our prayers; and focus on Spirit-inspired 'targets' of need to bring victory and breakthrough. Thank you, James, for this deep yet practical guidebook for prayer. Let us join together in a marvelous symphony of intercession that rises to the throne of God and returns to earth in His glory, powerfully transforming hearts and nations."

—*Joshua Mills*
Recording artist, keynote conference speaker, and author of more than twenty books, including *Moving in Glory Realms*

"In *Strike the Mark*, James Goll shares deep insights and essential principles drawn from a lifetime of prayer—from the time he was a young boy walking along the railroad tracks near his home just talking with Jesus to discovering his calling as a prophetic intercessor, prayerwalking on the walls of Jerusalem, and inviting believers to pray together for their neighborhoods via Periscope. This book will show you how to find your specific place and anointing in prayer and what it means to join with other believers in powerful agreement to bring God's purposes to earth. Each chapter builds on the next, leading you to pray from the victorious perspective of the finished work of Christ. *Strike the Mark* hits the target on what it means to be devoted to prayer (see Acts 2:42) and release the destiny of people and nations."

—*Dr. Kynan Bridges*
Senior pastor, Grace & Peace Global Fellowship, Tampa, Florida
Author, *The Power of Prophetic Prayer*, *90 Days of Prayer Power*, and
School of the Miraculous (October 2019)

STRIKE
THE
MARK

POWERFULLY TARGETED PRAYERS
FOR VICTORY AND BREAKTHROUGH

JAMES W. GOLL

WHITAKER
HOUSE

Boldface type in the Scripture quotations indicates the author's emphasis.

STRIKE THE MARK:
Powerfully Targeted Prayers for Victory and Breakthrough

James W. Goll
God Encounters Ministries
P.O. Box 1653
Franklin, TN 37065
www.godencounters.com • www.prayerstorm.com
www.compassionacts.com • www.GETeSchool.com
info@godencounters.com • inviteJames@gmail.com

ISBN: 978-1-64123-295-1
eBook ISBN: 978-1-64123-296-8
Printed in the United States of America

Whitaker House
1030 Hunt Valley Circle
New Kensington, PA 15068
www.whitakerhouse.com

Library of Congress Cataloging-in-Publication Data (Pending)

1 2 3 4 5 6 7 8 9 10 11 26 25 24 23 22 21 20 19

DEDICATION

For every book or message I compose, key people have contributed significant deposits into my mind and heart in the developmental stages. This book is no exception.

I met Mike Bickle when he was an eighteen-year-old Presbyterian and I was a twenty-year-old Methodist, not knowing that fifteen years later, I would begin serving for a decade on a vibrant church staff that he would lead. I found myself in a diversity of church gatherings, including congregational teaching assemblies, conferences, leadership times, and, of course, prayer meetings. If you served with Mike Bickle, you were in prayer meetings! I was on his ministry staff prior to the establishment of the International House of Prayer, which Mike founded. The church fellowship he led hosted morning, noon, and night prayer meetings for over ten years.

Mike Bickle has impacted my life in many significant ways, but the greatest imprint he has made on me comes from his consistent example of praying the Word of God. This man is truly one of this generation's "Generals of Prayer."

Therefore, it is my honor to dedicate this book on prayer to my friend, the Lord's servant, Mike Bickle.

"The prayer of a righteous person is powerful and effective."
—James 5:16 (NIV)

CONTENTS

FOREWORD

Prayers that *Strike the Mark* are guided by and endowed with the power of the Holy Spirit to accomplish the will and the Word of God. As faithful prayer warriors align with God's heart, they focus on "prayer targets," under the direction of the Holy Spirit, in order to partner with Jesus in prayer that results in victory and breakthrough. Such prayer warriors, relentlessly reminding God of His Word, call forth heavenly intervention so that the earth will one day be filled with the knowledge of the glory of the Lord.

Prayer always precedes the release of God's promises and purposes. According to Luke 2, before the first coming of Jesus the Messiah, there was a devout man named Simeon and a prophetess named Anna who were looking and praying for His coming. Their ministry of prayer and fasting was used by the Lord to confirm the fulfillment of the promise of a Redeemer. Likewise, before the second coming of Jesus, the Holy Spirit is raising up a global company of men and women who meditate upon the Scriptures, minister to the Lord, and intercede in unity with His heart and plan. Collectively, their spiritual sacrifices rise before the throne of God as a great concert of prayer.

For years, I have taught on the "harp and bowl" model of worship and prayer as depicted in Revelation 5:8. Worshipping intercessors and praying worshippers are being united in this generation to "win for the Lamb the rewards of His suffering," as the centuries-old cry goes. Like many of you, I long to see the day when the Spirit and the bride of Christ are in agreement so that all believers will declare, *"Even so, come, Lord Jesus!"* (Revelation 22:20).

I have known James Goll for over forty years. He served on the staff of the church that I pastored in the 1980s and '90s. I have witnessed his zeal and faithfulness to engage in prayer and to teach about prayer in a consistent way over many years. My friend James and I have walked through many peaks and valleys, and, by the grace of God, we have "kept our hand to the plow" (see Luke 9:62) in seeking to motivate, recruit, train, and mobilize intercessors for the great end-time revival. We both long to be "worshippers of God and deliverers of men."

James has not only been a person of prayer for years, but he is also one who has been given the grace of God to articulate and instruct people in the will, the Word, and the ways of God. In *Strike the Mark*, he includes chapters such as "The Orchestra of Prayer," "Coming into Agreement," and "Reminding God of His Word." This book will provide many practical insights into more effective prayer—prayer that is energized by a relationship with our most beautiful Lord Jesus and that is anchored in a victorious perspective.

It is a joy for me to commend to you this new equipping tool, *Strike the Mark*, for the Lord's prayer army.

—*Mike Bickle*
International House of Prayer of Kansas City
Author of a number of books, including *Growing in the Prophetic* and
Growing in Prayer

ACKNOWLEDGMENTS

It is an amazing honor to be an author. It is also a lot of hard work, with endless hours spent in study, research, presentation, writing, editing, reediting, and clarifying points so that others may "read the vision and run with it." You have heard the saying, "It takes a village." Well, it definitely takes a dedicated team of people to compose and publish a book!

I wish to acknowledge the teaching influences of both Mike Bickle and Dutch Sheets. The blend of their meaty content has helped to shape *Strike the Mark*. I also want to extend gratitude to the staff and team at Whitaker House and Anchor Distributors. This is now my fourth book to be published by this devoted publishing company. Within the staff of Whitaker House, I have had the distinct honor of working with Lois Puglisi as a premier editor. What an honor to be assisted by some of the best, and this dear lady is among the best editors I have ever worked with—and that includes a lot of sharp people. Thank you, Lois, and the Whitaker House team!

My constant writing assistant has been Kathy Deering. Surely, this dear woman of God will receive hundreds of gold stars for her patient and diligent efforts. She must have been touched by an angel and given an assignment. Perhaps the dialogue went something like this: "You see that man over there? He bites off more than he can chew! He really needs a lot of help. And it is recorded in heaven's prayer books that you have stated, 'Here am I. Use me, Lord!' Well, dear, we are cashing in on your offer. Go help him; yes, again. Yes, again and again."

Now, I doubt that conversation actually took place, but with a heart of gratitude, I wish to especially acknowledge Kathy as the decipherer and shaper of materials both old and new. You are an angel sent from heaven to me, and without your help, this book and many others would not be impacting the lives of hungry believers around the world today. Thank you!

INTRODUCTION: CALLING FORTH GOD'S GLORY

I awoke suddenly out of a vibrant dream that was filled with lightning. (Although this happened years ago, I remember it as if it were yesterday.) One lightning bolt after another exploded before my eyes—continual, splintering, powerful lightning bolts from heaven to earth. No people. No words. Just incessant light, action, sound.

When I woke up from this intense, Holy-Spirit-saturated dream, the whole room still crackled with God's electric presence. I lingered in that presence for twenty minutes or so before it dissipated. As I lay there musing, *What in the world was that about?* I saw "Job 36:32" spelled out in large, illuminated letters that were two or three feet tall. I turned on the light and found Job 36:32 in my Bible. I remember thinking dubiously that I rarely seemed to get anything out of the book of Job, but then I read this: *"He covers His hands with the lightning, and commands it to strike the mark"* (Job 36:32 NASB).

Lightning-fast, I made the connection. Lightning was "striking the mark," just as our God-directed intercessory prayers do. And everything fit together even better when I considered the huge role that such prayer had been playing in my life at that time. For starters, the dream occurred while I was staying in a suburb of Toronto on the last night of a Vineyard church conference called "Fire on the Altar," at which I was teaching about intercessory prayer. Prior to that, God had put me through ninety days of prayerful seclusion during which I had prayed in tongues for six to twelve hours a day. I had been sequestered in my home for three months straight, not doing any public ministry, but rather focusing on praying and singing in the Spirit. By the end of that time, I had grown so accustomed to praying in the secret place that I did not know whether I wanted to come out and engage in typical ministry again.

Another connection did not become clear until a few weeks later, when what is now known as the Toronto Blessing began. Yes, the first evidence of that special outpouring of the Holy Spirit occurred at the end of the very next month following my dream. I am convinced that what happened in Toronto could not have happened without the persistent, intercessory prayers of many, many people around the world, including mine.

Collectively, I believe our intercession had released the flashing forth of God's "glorious lightning" and directed it to hit specific targets of need. It really happened just as the verse from Job says: *"He covers His hands with the lightning, and commands it to strike the mark."*

The verse that follows is also interesting. It comments on the response to what has happened in verse 32: *"Its noise declares His presence"* (verse 33 NASB). Prayer creates lightning strikes from heaven—and thunder is the corresponding "sound" of that lightning. Prayer creates a thundering noise that declares God's presence. Thus, prayer produces a sound—more than that, a combination of sounds. In chapter one of this book, we will see how prayer is like the harmonious music of an orchestra.

A PLACE OF MEETING

People of prayer often work behind the scenes. While others in ministry work in plain view, they work in the "back room," in secret. Their prayerful intercession creates a place of meeting between God and men and women. In the midst of intercession, God lights upon the person praying and moves them from the natural to the supernatural. Empowered by God, the intercessor has the ability to cut down enemy forces and pick out targets for God's lightning bolts of glory. Prayers that "strike the mark" are prayers authorized by the Holy Spirit and endowed with divine power to accomplish the will of God.

In other words, intercession is our invitation to call forth the glory that is on God's hands in heaven and invite it to invade our space on earth. It is a high privilege to pray prayers that strike the mark. You and I have the great honor of being called to "paint targets" on our cities, on our churches and ministries, on our family members, on the modern-day Sauls in our lives (our persecutors), and even on ourselves. In prayer, we may target the United States government, the state of Tennessee, the city of Los Angeles, particular missionary and relief organizations, people we hear about in the news, people in authority, and much more.

"EXTREME PRAYER"

I keep using the word *target*, both as a noun and as a verb, because it is part of the definition of the Hebrew root word *paga*, which English-speakers often translate as "intercede." *Paga* generally indicates "to meet," but its shades of meaning include "to light upon by chance," "to fall upon," "to attack," "to strike down," and "to cut down"—as well as "to strike the mark." The word *paga* does not relate only to prayer, but the various nuances of its meaning can help us understand the dimensions of intercessory prayer.

The meaning of *paga* is very similar to the English word *intercede*, which comes from the Latin and means "to go between" (*inter*: between; *cedere*: to go), to act between parties with a view to reconciling those who differ or contend, to plead in favor of another, to interpose, to get involved in solving a problem, to step into the gap when needed, to meet with, or to mediate.

In a real way, you could call intercession "extreme prayer," because it brings together extreme needs with the extraordinary power of God—bridging those two extremes. By inserting ourselves into the gap between God and a need, we help to bring about a work of grace, calling upon the Holy Spirit, our Helper, who is standing by ready to move us from finite ability to infinite ability, enabling us to take hold of situations and help accomplish the will of God.

Here are some Scripture passages that demonstrate the distinctive meanings of the Hebrew word *paga*:

> You **meet** [paga] him who rejoices in doing righteousness, who remembers You in Your ways. (Isaiah 64:5 NASB)

> And Jacob went out from Beersheba, and went toward Haran. And he **lighted upon** [paga] a certain place, and tarried there all night, because the sun was set; and he took of the stones of that place, and put them for his pillows, and lay down in that place to sleep. And he dreamed, and behold a ladder set up on the earth, and the top of it reached to heaven: and behold the angels of God ascending and descending on it. And, behold, the LORD stood above it, and said, I am the LORD God of Abraham thy father, and the God of Isaac: the land whereon thou liest, to thee will I give it, and to thy seed.... And, behold, I am with thee, and will keep thee in all places whither thou goest, and will bring thee again into this land; for I will not leave thee, until I have done that which I have spoken to thee of. And Jacob awaked out of his sleep, and he said, Surely the LORD is in this place; and I knew it not. And he was afraid, and said, How dreadful is this place! this is none other but the house of God, and this is the gate of heaven.
> (Genesis 28:10–13, 15–17 KJV)

> And they mourned, and wept, and fasted until even, for Saul, and for Jonathan his son, and for the people of the LORD, and for the house of Israel; because they were fallen by the sword. And David said unto the young man that told him, Whence art thou? And he answered, I am the son of a stranger, an Amalekite. And David said unto him, How wast thou not afraid to stretch forth thine hand to destroy the LORD's anointed? And David called one of the young men, and said, Go near, and **fall upon** [paga] him. And he

smote him that he died.

(2 Samuel 1:12–15 KJV; see also 1 Samuel 22:17–18)

*We all, like sheep, have gone astray, each of us has turned to our
own way; and the LORD* **has laid** *[paga] on him the iniquity of us
all.… Therefore I will give him a portion among the great, and he
will divide the spoils with the strong, because he poured out his life
unto death, and was numbered with the transgressors. For he bore
the sin of many, and* **made intercession** *[paga] for the transgressors.* (Isaiah 53:6, 12 NIV)

The above passage from Isaiah refers to the Messiah, Jesus. It
describes how intercession reached its fullest and most profound
expression when our sins were "laid upon" Jesus. Jesus was able to
fully identify with us, having had the totality of our sinful condition
placed upon Him. And as the Scapegoat, He carried it far away. (See
Leviticus 16:1–22.)

There is an aspect of this form of intercession into which we, as the
body of Christ, can enter. Paul writes about filling up in his flesh what
is still lacking in regard to Christ's afflictions *"for the sake of His body,
which is the church"* (Colossians 1:24).

According to these ways of understanding *paga,* or intercession,
praying believers present targets so that the Holy Spirit can take a
measure of heaven's glory and send it forth to strike the mark. What
an invitation to pray prayers that strike the mark!

YOU ARE QUALIFIED

We have been invited to draw God's attention to specific places
where He can intervene. On the cross, Jesus already accomplished the
ultimate answer to all of our prayers, but God awaits our specific invitation to come into each scene.

You may say, "I am not qualified for this. I am not an apostle…I am
not a prophet…I don't think I'm even very sharp." But I say, "You *are*
qualified." If you are a believer in the Lord Jesus Christ, He has given

you both authority and power over the enemy. He is waiting for you to follow Him as He uses your Spirit-breathed prayers to gain victory over the foe and bring blessings to His people! Are you ready?

1

THE ORCHESTRA OF PRAYER

*"He [King Hezekiah] organized Levites at the Temple into
an orchestral group, using cymbals, psalteries, and harps.
This was in accordance with the directions of David and the
prophets Gad and Nathan, who had received their
instructions from the Lord. The priests formed a trumpet corps.
Then Hezekiah ordered the burnt offering to be placed upon the
altar, and as the sacrifice began, the instruments of music began
to play the songs of the Lord, accompanied by the trumpets.
Throughout the entire ceremony everyone worshiped the Lord
as the singers sang and the trumpets blew. Afterwards the king
and his aides bowed low before the Lord in worship. Then King
Hezekiah ordered the Levites to sing before the Lord some of the
psalms of David and of the prophet Asaph, which they gladly did,
and bowed their heads and worshiped."*
—2 Chronicles 29:25–30 (TLB)

I want to make one thing as clear as possible from the beginning:
prayer cannot be defined simplistically. It is more like symphonic
music, played harmoniously by many different instruments, than a
single trumpet blast.

I recently had the joy of attending a performance of the Nashville
Concerto Orchestra. It was marvelous. I felt I was in an ecstatic

atmosphere where the sounds of heaven were being released on earth. It was all the more delightful for me because, among the orchestra members, my daughter-in-law, Pearl Fernando Goll, wife of my son Tyler, was beautifully playing the violin. The whole sound ebbed and flowed like the tide as the delicate notes of the oboe were followed by the thunderous waves of the drums, all held together by layers of strings. It was seamless, and yet each instrument had its unique and particular part to play in making the music.

In the same way that it takes all kinds of musical sounds to make up an orchestra, it takes all kinds of prayers to respond to our Conductor, Jesus Christ Himself. That is why Ephesians 6:18 uses this particular wording: *"Praying always with all prayer and supplication,"* or *"...all kinds of prayers"* (NIV). The score is the written Word of God. The tempo is set and moderated by the Holy Spirit. The instruments are played by you and me—and we get better with intentional practice.

Our instruments of prayer vary as greatly as the instruments in an orchestra do. Just as an orchestra consists of groups of woodwinds, strings, brass, and percussion instruments, so our instruments of prayer may be plucked, strummed, bowed, blown into, pounded on, shouted, or whispered. Note, as well, that our chorus of prayer often consists of "movements," such as praise, worship, and intercessory prayers.

TWELVE DIVERSE SOUNDS OF PRAYER

The point is this: each and every one of us has a part to play in God's orchestra of prayer. What is your special sound? What instrument do you play?

I have identified twelve distinct "sounds" that come forth in the orchestra of prayer. They are as follows (these are by no means rigid categories): (1) thanksgiving; (2) high praise; (3) worship; (4) dedication, or consecration; (5) prayers of commitment; (6) prayers of petition; (7) prayers of intercession; (8) prayers of supplication; (9) prayers of command; (10) prayers that decree a blessing; (11) prayers that thwart the enemy; and (12) persistent prayers. Let's explore their distinct contributions.

THANKSGIVING

Prayers of thanksgiving are like the first movement in a symphony. They open the way to a concert of worship and intercession. The psalmist declares, *"Enter His gates with thanksgiving"* (Psalm 100:4 NASB), and that is what we do. That is what happened for the grateful leper in Luke 17:11–19. According to Old Testament law, lepers were supposed to declare, "Unclean! Unclean!" wherever they went (see Leviticus 13:45), and they were expected to stay away from other people. But ten lepers approached Jesus for healing. Jesus sent them to the priests so that their cleansing from the disease could be verified—and they were healed as they went. Nine of them continued on their way, incredulous and in high spirits. But one turned around and came back to express his thanks directly to the rabbi whose power had healed him. He is the one whose thankful heart opened the way to more liberty, joy, and healing. The others were cleansed—but he was made whole. Jesus told him, *"Thy faith hath made thee whole"* (Luke 17:19 KJV). Thanksgiving is an important quality of a healthy, whole person.

HIGH PRAISE

What follows *"Enter His gates with thanksgiving..."*? It is *"...and* [go into] *His courts with praise"* (Psalm 100:4 NASB). Thanksgiving and praise are not quite the same thing. There is a progression. First, we thank God for His goodness: *"For the LORD is good"* (verse 5). Then, we praise Him for His greatness: *"Great is the LORD, and greatly to be praised"* (Psalm 48:1). Always remember that praise is one of the highest weapons of spiritual warfare. Praise opens prison doors and sets the captives free.

WORSHIP

Following thanksgiving and praise, we move into heartfelt worship. Despite the fact that I am comparing these aspects of prayer to instruments in an orchestra, in reality, worship pertains less to music—which is how we tend to think of it in a contemporary church context—and more to an inner attitude of the heart. To worship is to bow down, to kneel, to prostrate oneself. Another psalm gives expression to what I'm trying to describe here:

> *Oh come, let us worship and bow down; let us kneel before the* LORD *our Maker. For He is our God, and we are the people of His pasture, and the sheep of His hand.* (Psalm 95:6–7)

We might begin with joyful shouting, as Psalm 95 encourages us in its first few verses, because God is so great. Our expressions of praise, which can be chosen as an act of the will, may then lead us into heartfelt worship as the ultimate expression of surrender to God. Worship, according to the first point of the Westminster Shorter Catechism, is "the chief end of man." It is foundational to our faith, with or without audible musical notes.

DEDICATION (CONSECRATION)

Building on what has come before, we present ourselves to God. We *"present* [our] *bodies a living and holy sacrifice, acceptable to God, which is* [our] *spiritual service of worship"* (Romans 12:1 NASB). This enables us to enter into the High Priestly Prayer of Jesus in John 17 as we are set apart for the Lord and sanctified. He prayed to the Father, *"For their sakes I sanctify Myself, that they themselves also may be sanctified in truth"* (John 17:19 NASB).

Our prayers of consecration are a lovely sound to the Lord's ears. He loves to hear "saving grace" prayers, too, but our dedication and consecration prayers show Him that we know we are not our own, that we were bought with a price. "I surrender all" resounds from the orchestra of prayer. Jesus Christ is our Master and Lord!

PRAYERS OF COMMITMENT

As we progress, our prayers of dedication and consecration lead to prayers of commitment, and we say, as the psalmist did, *"Into Your hand I commit my spirit; You have redeemed me, O* LORD *God of truth"* (Psalm 31:5). As we commit ourselves to Him, we rest in faith-filled trust. He will take care of us, down to the smallest detail of our lives.

"Commit everything you do to the L*ord. Trust him, and he will help you"* (Psalm 37:5 n*lt*).

Committing is an act; trust is an attitude. Whenever your load becomes too heavy, you cast your burden onto the Lord. (See 1 Peter 5:7.) You commit it to Him. And then you leave it with Him; you trust Him with it. You give it and then leave it.

I think of the serene summer night in Dallas at the Cotton Bowl Stadium, where I was attending Campus Crusade for Christ's Explo '72 conference. The renowned evangelist Billy Graham spoke a piercing message about personal commitment to Christ. As a result both of the preached message and the convicting work of the Holy Spirit, I stood to my feet to dedicate my life to full-time Christian service. It was one of the best decisions I have ever made, one that has stuck for over forty-five years! I am sure that my simple prayer of consecration released a soothing orchestral sound to the Lord's ears.

PRAYERS OF PETITION

Many times, we pray simple prayers of petition in addition to prayers of commitment. We can expect each of our prayers to be answered—if they line up with the will of God. *"Now this is the confidence that we have in Him, that if we ask anything according to His will, He hears us"* (1 John 5:14). I like to say it this way: God came up with the original "World Wide Web." His "WWW" consists of His will, His Word, and His ways.

When you pray, do you ask the Bible way? *"Therefore I say to you, whatever things you ask when you pray, believe that you receive them, and you will have them"* (Mark 11:24). This does not mean that you will have everything you fervently desire, but that you will align your desires with His as you walk in increasing holiness.

PRAYERS OF INTERCESSION

At last, we reach intercessory prayer, the primary topic of this book. Did you know that all those different "sounds" of prayer must be heard first? We have to come through the gates with praise before we can enter into the Most Holy Place.

God looks among His people for intercessors—and they are hard to find: *"I looked for someone among them who would build up the wall and stand before me in the gap on behalf of the land…, but I found no one"* (Ezekiel 22:30 NIV).

Intercession is not "devotional prayer." That form of prayer should have been covered already in your earlier time of communion with the Lord. Intercession is making prayers of petition on behalf of others, standing in the gap between man's imperfection and God's perfection. We confess the iniquity of others as if it is our own and we ask for God's mercy. (See, for example, Isaiah 59:2–15.) What a high honor it is, a labor of love, to be allowed to stand in the gap on behalf of other people!

PRAYERS OF SUPPLICATION

The apostle James tells us that *"mercy triumphs over judgment"* (James 2:13). To pray according to mercy is always to pray according to God's heart. This is much more difficult than it sounds—even impossible. In fact, you cannot lift up a cry for mercy without receiving God's grace to do so. Ask for the *"spirit of grace and supplication"*: *"And I will pour out on the house of David and the inhabitants of Jerusalem a spirit of grace and supplication. They will look on me, the one they have pierced, and they will mourn for him as one mourns for an only child, and grieve bitterly for him as one grieves for a firstborn son"* (Zechariah 12:10 NIV).

"Let us therefore come boldly unto the throne of grace, that we may obtain mercy, and find grace to help in time of need" (Hebrews 4:16 KJV). We cannot come boldly to the throne of grace in our own human strength. We must come with heartfelt thanksgiving, praise, and worship, surrendering our own agendas. Then we can receive His heart of mercy and pray according to His will.

PRAYERS OF COMMAND

Once in a while, coming "boldly" entails uttering commanding words of prayer, as Joshua did when he spoke to the Lord and then released commands to the sun and the moon, so that the sun stood still for an entire day. (See Joshua 10:12–15.) It takes a profound gift of faith to do something like that.

John Wimber, founder of the Vineyard church movement, taught about the five-stage healing model. One of his personal ministry prayers was the prayer of command in which he spoke to the illness, "Be gone!"

The prayer of command is declarative in nature. Even though you may not play that "instrument" regularly in the prayer orchestra, it is important to know that it is a biblical option.

PRAYERS THAT DECREE A BLESSING

Much more often, we utter prayers of blessing, even decreeing specific blessings. We can bless others with these words, which the Lord gave to Moses:

> And the LORD spoke to Moses, saying: "Speak to Aaron and his sons, saying, 'This is the way you shall bless the children of Israel. Say to them: "The LORD bless you and keep you; the LORD make His face shine upon you, and be gracious to you; the LORD lift up His countenance upon you, and give you peace."'"
>
> (Numbers 6:22–26)

This is how God releases His blessings on His people: "So they shall put ["invoke" NKJV marginal note] My name on the children of Israel, and I will bless them" (Numbers 6:27). Remember this key point: we are part of a speech-activated kingdom. When, fueled by the gift of faith, you decree something that is according to the will, Word, and ways of God, all things are possible! (See, for example, Matthew 19:26.)

PRAYERS THAT THWART THE ENEMY

Can we utter prayers that denounce or limit the powers of darkness? Can we bind Satan from continuing his work? Well, Jesus illustrated the believer's power to do so when He cursed a fig tree that was not bearing fruit, after which it withered and died. (See Matthew

21:18–22.) This is like a prayer of command coupled with righteousness and faith. Jesus inspected the tree and found no figs, only leaves, on it. It had given the external appearance of being fruitful, but upon closer examination, it proved to be unproductive.

This is the kind of prayer that draws a line in the sand and says, "Enough is enough. No more!" Although it was used by Jesus, this form of prayer should be exercised with wisdom and caution. It requires clear discernment and faith and should be employed only after confirmation from God.

PERSISTENT PRAYERS

The final sound in the orchestra of prayer is one of persistence. The orchestra keeps on playing even if the lights go out. There is the familiar parable in the book of Luke about the persistent widow whose appeal to the judge was answered only because she would not let it go. (See Luke 18:1–8.) Earlier in Luke, Jesus told another parable about a friend whose persistent entreaties produced results. (See Luke 11:5–8.) The bottom line is this:

> *Keep on asking, and you will receive what you ask for. Keep on seeking, and you will find. Keep on knocking, and the door will be opened to you. For everyone who asks, receives. Everyone who seeks, finds. And to everyone who knocks, the door will be opened.* (Luke 11:9–10 NLT)

Keep on praying. Don't give up. The more you pray, the more God will keep on drawing you into His heart. You and I have been called to be enforcers of the kingdom of light over the (temporary) kingdom of darkness. Giving up is not an option!

OUTLINE OF THE ORCHESTRA

Let me summarize this picture of the orchestra of prayer by giving you a list of points about intercessory prayer that I gleaned years ago from my friend Mike Bickle, founder of the International House of

Prayer in Kansas City, Missouri. Briefly stated, intercessory prayer has five aspects:

1. Personal petitions (asking for circumstances in your life to change)

2. Personal devotion (asking for spiritual growth, communion with God, and worship)

3. Meditation on God's Word (turning God's Word into a conversation with Jesus)

4. Intercession for God's corporate purpose (watching over the people of God) (see, for example, 1 Thessalonians 3:10; Isaiah 62:6–7; Luke 18:7–8)

5. Intercession for specific individuals (see, for example, 2 Corinthians 1:11; Ephesians 6:18–19; Philippians 1:19)

Each of these aspects of intercessory prayer requires certain foundational conditions if the prayer is to be effective. To keep us aiming in the right direction, here are ten of these important conditions with some supporting Scriptures:

1. Faith (see Mark 11:23–24; Matthew 21:21–22)

2. Persistence (see Luke 18:1–8; Matthew 7:7–11; Isaiah 30:18–19; 62:6–7; Luke 11:5–13)

3. Holy life (Psalm 66:18; Isaiah 59:1–2; 1 John 3:19–22)

4. Honor for spouse (1 Peter 3:7)

5. Following the will of God (1 John 5:14–15)

6. Praying in the name of Jesus (John 14:13–14; 26; 16:23–24)

7. Pure motives (James 4:2–3)

8. Boldness (Hebrews 4:16)

9. Forgiveness (Matthew 6:15)

10. Unity, praying in agreement (Matthew 18:19–20; 5:23–24)

To underline the importance of our intercession—our persistent asking, seeking, and knocking on the door of heaven—Jesus affirmed the Father's expansive generosity, saying:

> *So I say to you, ask, and it will be given to you; seek, and you will find; knock, and it will be opened to you. For everyone who asks receives, and he who seeks finds, and to him who knocks it will be opened. If a son asks for bread from any father among you, will he give him a stone? Or if he asks for a fish, will he give him a serpent instead of a fish? Or if he asks for an egg, will he offer him a scorpion? If you then, being evil, know how to give good gifts to your children, how much more will your heavenly Father give the Holy Spirit to those who ask Him!* (Luke 11:9–13)

If you will line up your life and your prayers with God's will, Word, and ways, your patient perseverance will be rewarded. God will open His heavenly storehouse to meet the need you have been praying about. Your holy, believing, persistent prayers will strike the mark!

TARGET PRACTICE

Almighty God, in Jesus's great name, I thank You that the fervent prayer of a righteous believer prevails! By the grace of God, I am adding these various sounds of prayer into my understanding. Holy Spirit, guide and direct me in choosing which instrument should be selected at the appropriate time and how to play it. I praise and thank You that You are teaching me how to release prayers that will strike the mark without fail. Amen. (See James 5:16.)

2

COMING INTO AGREEMENT

"I will give you the keys of the kingdom of heaven; and whatever
you bind on earth shall have been bound in heaven, and whatever
you loose on earth shall have been loosed in heaven."
—Matthew 16:19 (NASB)

Jesus told us to persist—continuously and tirelessly—in asking, seeking, and knocking on the doors of heaven. I quoted His specific words at the end of the previous chapter. The *New Living Translation* emphasizes the ongoing action in that passage:

> And so I tell you, **keep on** asking, and you will receive what you ask for. **Keep on** seeking, and you will find. **Keep on** knocking, and the door will be opened to you. For everyone who asks, receives. Everyone who seeks, finds. And to everyone who knocks, the door will be opened. (Luke 11:9–10 NLT)

Keep on doing it. Keep on keeping on. Keep on praying! I also want to urge you to keep on *coming*—keep coming to God and keep coming into agreement with Him as well as with your brothers and sisters who pray alongside you. If you are still coming, it means you have not yet arrived, and that is OK. It is the *keeping on* that is important as we grow spiritually and learn more about what it means to ask, seek, and knock in agreement with God and others.

HARMONIOUS SOUNDS REACH HEAVEN

In chapter 1, I used an orchestra metaphor to describe the way our individual "instruments" of prayer blend together into one magnificent sound. When the instruments play together—in agreement with each other—the sound penetrates beyond the immediate vicinity into heaven itself. And Jesus says that whatever you declare from your position on earth will be matched by a response from heaven. He also says that it only takes two or three people praying in agreement to make a big difference:

> *Truly I tell you, whatever you bind on earth will be bound in heaven, and whatever you loose on earth will be loosed in heaven. Again, truly I tell you that if two of you on earth agree about anything they ask for, it will be done for them by my Father in heaven. For where two or three gather in my name, there am I with them.*
>
> (Matthew 18:18–20 NIV)

What does it take to come into agreement? Could it be more than simply clasping hands and saying, "Brother/Sister, let's agree on this together"? The prayer of agreement happens when the sections of God's orchestra, well-practiced and with their instruments finely tuned, play together in harmony, without dissonance. Within the body of Christ, this means building strong relationships with one another. Prayer is a natural by-product of believers who are united in Christ.

What unites us? Our faith. John writes, *"For whatever is born of God overcomes the world; and this is the victory that has overcome the world—our faith"* (1 John 5:4 NASB).

What will overcome the world? *Our* faith. Not *my* faith or some good-sounding prayers. Our *collective* faith. Pulling together in agreement, first with God and then with each other, we gain the victory. The value and priority of developing prayer partnerships and a committed community of prayer cannot be overstated.

LET US BREAK BREAD TOGETHER

What does prayerful unity look like? We get a glimpse of it in descriptions of the life of the early church: *"All the believers devoted themselves to the apostles' teaching, and to fellowship, and to sharing in meals (including the Lord's Supper), and to prayer"* (Acts 2:42 NLT). Sharing our lives in an ongoing way makes us more like Jesus, doesn't it? To do this, we have to forgive and serve and love each other.

Our corporate prayer life is both formal and informal, scheduled and spontaneous. We can pray everywhere, not only in worship services. We may begin to appreciate the model that Paul laid out for the church when he wrote, *"Pray in the Spirit on **all** occasions with **all** kinds of prayers and requests. With this in mind, be alert and **always keep on** praying for **all** the Lord's people"* (Ephesians 6:18 NIV).

There are many different but thoroughly biblical expressions of prayer. Just think of the variety of sports, games, and activities that are available in the world, with different rules for each game. It is much the same with intercessory prayer. There are as many different sets of "rules," guidelines, and ways of "scoring" as there are types of prayer and combinations of people praying.

CLARITY BEFORE AGREEMENT

In order to access heaven together (vertical dimension), we must learn what it takes to relate to other people in effective ways (horizontal dimension). Before coming into agreement with others in prayer, therefore, we need wisdom to know what kind of situation we are entering into. We may need "environmental" and cultural information as much as spiritual knowledge.

Different types of prayer are appropriate at different times, and we are not necessarily called to engage in all of them in one gathering. An obvious example would be something like this: Let's say you are going into a scheduled prayer meeting at your church. Maybe the topic of prayer—a national crisis, for instance—has been announced beforehand. Your personal inclination might be to go in there with all your guns blazing to blast the devil off the planet; this stuff makes you so angry at him. But you might want to "case out" the atmosphere of the meeting first. What if it is a "harp and bowl," worship-based prayer meeting? Your anti-devil approach just might be out of place. You might find it slow getting into the worship at first, but your job is to come into agreement with the others—not only in terms of subject matter but also in terms of style of worship and prayer.

I have come up with some questions you can ask yourself as you assess a prayer meeting and discern your appropriate level of involvement. For starters, ask yourself:

+ Is this a "Spirit-filled believers'" prayer gathering? (Is it a traditional church setting, evangelical, or charismatic?)

+ Is there room for the "uninitiated"? (By this, I mean people who are "born again" but not yet baptized in or interested in things of the Holy Spirit.)

+ Is this an open meeting or a closed, invitation-only gathering?

+ Have targeted prayer goals been established or will the meeting be led spontaneously?

+ Is this an interdenominational group or a group of relationally joined prayer partners?

+ Has relational unity been cultivated over a period of time? (This allows for greater authority in prayer.)

+ Are you properly discerning your sphere of authority in this place and at this time? (Some people, not understanding this point, may launch into prayer to, say, break down communism over China when their sphere of true authority is over their family, job, or city. They have not learned that only as we are faithful with our known sphere of authority will God develop us and grant us a greater measure of authority over broader matters.)

Here are some additional basic questions to consider:

+ Are the gifts of the Spirit free to operate here?[1]

+ Would it be all right to weep, groan, and travail in prayer here?[2]

+ Is loud corporate praying appropriate here?

+ Are the people here familiar with the contemplative traditions of prayer?[3]

+ Do the believers here engage in times of silence or "soaking" worship?[4]

Styles of worship and prayer can be cultural preferences, not only across denominational lines but also ethnic and national lines. When I go into Asian countries, I am plunged into prayer situations in which the people all pray aloud together at the same time. Even though it is noisy, it is very much under control. They just assume that is how you are supposed to pray, even if some of their guests find it hard to adjust to at first. (Frankly, I greatly appreciate this style of prayer and I wish that more of the Western church would engage in it.)

In other places, groups will praise and praise and praise, and you wonder when they are going to shift into something else. Then they move into "soaking" in the presence of God. If you are a prayer warrior and find yourself in this situation, you might become frustrated. Please understand that yours is not the only way of interceding. The people at such meetings may be getting results from all their praising, because praise is a weapon against the enemy. Or, they may be increasing in the spirit of revelation by waiting on the Lord.

It is always a good idea to stick with your best weapons, and these groups might be doing just that. If you are going to come into

---

1. For an in-depth exploration of the gifts of the Spirit, see my book *Releasing Spiritual Gifts Today* (New Kensington, PA: Whitaker House, 2016).

2. For an in-depth exploration of travailing prayer, see my book *Praying with God's Heart: The Power and Purpose of Prophetic Intercession* (Grand Rapids, MI: Chosen Books, 2018), formerly titled *The Prophetic Intercessor*.

3. My book *The Lost Art of Practicing His Presence* (Shippensburg, PA: Destiny Image, 2007) expounds on this approach to prayer.

4. I included a section on the power of soaking worship in my book *Prayer Storm* (Shippensburg, PA: Destiny Image, 2013).

agreement with them in prayer, you will need to be adaptable enough to put down your battle-ax and become a worship warrior. This is especially important if you happen to be helping to lead the gathering. I have had to wear many different hats according to the requirements and responsibilities of different prayer gatherings.

Here are a few more strategic questions:

- Who is the leader? (The leader sets the tone and direction.)
- Is this what is known as a "watch of the Lord"? (This often involves many hours of long intercession, even all-night prayer vigils.)
- Should you be journaling your experience? (Do you record prayer requests, answers, and leadings of the Holy Spirit? Do you have an appointed scribe for your group who is in charge of keeping a journal?)
- Are you here to pray for those in authority? (This could be a prayer time focused on the government, spiritual leaders, or family members.)
- Are there conditions and biblical promises that you should review in order to be properly prepared? (Have assignments been given out ahead of time to the watchmen-intercessors? Is there a devotional time first?)

To be able to enter into a time of effective prayer that strikes the mark, you need to consider these questions and others. Learn to appreciate the fact that there are many valid biblical expressions of intercessory ministry with different strategies for implementation.

BEING BUILT TOGETHER INTO A RELATIONAL COMMUNITY

Jesus does not want you to pray alone all the time. Of course, you need to keep your focus vertical—on Him. However, as I have been sharing, your prayers will be hindered if you do not also work on the horizontal relational skills that will enable you to come into agreement with others in prayer.

Communication skills are the most important relational skills you can develop because prayer is communication with God, and the enemy knows it. Therefore, he tries to mess up our communication with God and with each other at every opportunity, planting lies and insinuations and accusations and half-truths. We need to capture those falsehoods and reject them. As Scripture says, "Catch us the foxes, the little foxes that spoil the vines, for our vines have tender grapes" (Song of Solomon 2:15).

Prayer ministries can begin well but fizzle in the end because of disruptions in the relationships between the members. It is all too easy for misunderstandings to arise. Perhaps a prayer effort was launched because of a particular project, so that the intercession is project-oriented. Once the project is accomplished, people should not continue praying in the same way. However, as the prayer gatherings continue, people's expectations for the group might now differ and communication among the members might become faulty. Urged on by the enemy, the members might allow their confusion to turn them against each other. Yet if the leader clearly communicates the new goal of the prayer meetings, such issues can be avoided or resolved more easily.

One of the most insidious "little foxes" is gossip. Have you ever been in a prayer meeting where a request for prayer or a follow-up to prayer becomes nothing more than an excuse to gossip about somebody's problems? That is not prayer—and it is not helping anybody.

It can take a lifetime to learn how to honor other people with your thoughts and speech and to be slow to take offense, but it is definitely worth the effort. We want to be like Jesus, who could say, "The ruler of this world is coming, and he has nothing in Me" (John 14:30). He was referring to the devil; in Jesus's life, Satan could find no common ground on which to stand, no hidden sin by which he could trip Jesus up.

Difficulties, mistakes, failures, hurts, and offenses will occur in each of our lives. We must learn how to give and receive forgiveness, show compassion, and confront others lovingly with a goal of reconciliation. The blood of Jesus cleanses us *all* from *all* sin (see 1 John 1:9)—if we will allow it to do so.

In his epistle, James advises us to *"confess* [our] *sins to one another, and pray for one another so that* [we] *may be healed. The effective prayer of a righteous man can accomplish much"* (James 5:16 NASB). James enfolds prayer in a relational garment, underlining the importance of mutual, cleansing confession to answered prayer. We must relate to each other on the basis of mutual respect and honor before we can expect our prayers for healing and restoration to be answered.

It takes a concerted effort for believers to be built together into a unified body. We must be consecrated to Christ and dedicated to the task. More than being centered on our prayer assignments, we must be centered on Christ Himself. Believing in one another, we cover each other in love. We make it our aim to tame our tongues, to grow in the compassionate art of confronting each other in love, and to continue to walk in loyalty to God and to our brothers and sisters in Christ. The fruit is the power of agreement.

THE POWER OF AGREEMENT

Agreement is a wonderful by-product of lives that have been forged together in God's kingdom of righteousness, peace, and joy. (See Romans 14:17.) Our prayers bear fruit because "two or three" have gathered together in His name and have with one mind and heart prayed together. In fact, Scripture promises that God will be in our midst. We come into agreement with Him, and as we keep our eyes fixed on Him, He brings us into agreement with one another. This is heaven on earth. What could be more powerful than that?

We should not underestimate the *power* of agreement. Because God has placed His authority on humankind to work out His plan and purposes in the world, our corporate agreement with Him brings about His will on the earth. In other words, when, together, we agree with God about something, it is very likely to happen. (By the same token, if we agree with the enemy—*"the god of this world"* (2 Corinthians 4:4 NASB)—about something, even in ignorance, that too is likely to happen.)[5]

How can you discern whether or not you are consistently aligning yourself with God? By paying attention to your routine thought processes. Do you spend most of your time thinking about worldly concerns or do you daily and actively trust God to take care of your needs? How much are you communicating with Him? What is He telling you?

We enter into agreement by being connected with God and with each other, and we enter into this lifestyle by offering ourselves up to Him (and to one another) in the light of God's mercy. We reject the message of the world around us, which is to trust in ourselves and to "look out for number one." True agreement requires mutual humility and honor.

Helping each other conform to God's way of doing things makes us one. Who would want to be conformed to the tragic, condemnatory way of the world when you could be enjoying the light of God's approval and love? The Father sent His own Son to earth to bring us back to Himself. Let's go for it, surrendering all of our old ways of thinking and acting as He points them out to us. Along with Paul, I say:

> *Therefore, I urge you, brothers and sisters, in view of God's mercy, to offer your bodies as a living sacrifice, holy and pleasing to God— this is your true and proper worship. Do not conform to the pattern of this world, but be transformed by the renewing of your mind. Then you will be able to test and approve what God's will is—his good, pleasing and perfect will.* (Romans 12:1–2 NIV)

Then we can pray together the most powerful prayers of all. Look at the amazing power that was released when the early church prayed as one voice:

---

5. Ideas for this section come from the writings of the late John Wimber, founder of the Vineyard churches.

When they heard the report [about what had happened to Peter and John before the Sanhedrin], *all the believers lifted their voices together in prayer to God: "O Sovereign Lord, Creator of heaven and earth, the sea, and everything in them—you spoke long ago by the Holy Spirit through our ancestor David, your servant, saying, 'Why were the nations so angry? Why did they waste their time with futile plans? The kings of the earth prepared for battle; the rulers gathered together against the* Lord *and against his Messiah.' In fact, this has happened here in this very city! For Herod Antipas, Pontius Pilate the governor, the Gentiles, and the people of Israel were all united against Jesus, your holy servant, whom you anointed. But everything they did was determined beforehand according to your will. And now, O Lord, hear their threats, and give us, your servants, great boldness in preaching your word. Stretch out your hand with healing power; may miraculous signs and wonders be done through the name of your holy servant Jesus." After this prayer, the meeting place shook, and they were all filled with the Holy Spirit. Then they preached the word of God with boldness.* (Acts 4:24–31 nlt)

GOD'S HEART AND YOURS

Praying in agreement with God and each other starts with each one of us being as close as possible to the very heart of God. Do you love Jesus? Do you love the believers you have been joined with? Are you learning to lean into the heart of God Himself? Are you praying *to* God or *with* God? The first and primary Person with whom we are to come into agreement is, of course, God Himself. Your effectiveness in prayer will depend on how well your heart pulses in rhythm with the heartbeat of God.

There is no easy, "three-step" approach or methodology for coming into agreement. It takes time. It is relational. It calls for character. It necessitates love. It is a matter of the heart. First, each one of us comes into agreement with God Himself, and we maintain a desire to keep as close to Him as we can, setting aside our own agendas. Then, we put aside our prejudices and preconceived ideas and come into agreement with each other. When you learn to agree with God, then your agenda, your motivations, and even your assignments will change. Your mind will be transformed according to the will of God: *"Do not be conformed to this world, but be transformed by the renewing of your mind, that you may prove what is that good and acceptable and perfect will of God"* (Romans 12:2).

Only then can we be candidates to pray prayers that strike the mark!

TARGET PRACTICE

Heavenly Father, I come to You in Jesus's great name. I ask You to graft into my life Your wisdom concerning prayer. More than anything, I want to come into agreement with Your heart and learn to pray in accordance with Your will, Word, and ways. Help me to find two or three others with whom I may learn to walk in the power of prayers of agreement. Thank You. Amen.

3

THE FACES OF PRAYER

"I exhort first of all that supplications, prayers, intercessions, and giving of thanks be made for all men."
—1 Timothy 2:1

Although prayers that strike the mark have many "faces," or expressions, such prayer must be cohesive to be effective, as described in the previous chapter. We must come into agreement first with God and His Word, next with our spiritual leaders, and then with our fellow believers (one or two others, at least). We also need to come into agreement with ourselves. When we find that we are conflicted in mind or spirit, we must try to resolve those internal issues before we can present our requests to God in the most effectual way.

That being said, I want to be sure to add that our actual prayers do not need to be expressed in exactly the same manner. In fact, there is so much variety of expression in prayer, so many different and overlapping models and patterns, that I will be able to present only an overview of them in this chapter.

"WITH ALL PRAYER AND SUPPLICATION"

Let me begin by reminding you of five words from Ephesians 6:18: *"with all prayer and supplication."* This phrase is part of Paul's exhortation to believers to wear the full armor of God: *"Take the helmet of salvation, and the sword of the Spirit, which is the word of God; praying always* **with all prayer and supplication** *in the Spirit*" (Ephesians 6:17–18). Other versions of Scripture translate the phrase as follows: "*with all kinds of prayers and requests*" (NIV) and "*with all prayer and petition*" (NASB).

Paul is urging believers to pray all types of prayers and requests all the time. We should pray consistently, ceaselessly. This means that we may pray with all kinds of sounds (recalling the orchestra image)—and with no sounds at all. We may pray alone and we may pray in unity with others. We may pray in our native languages and also in the gift of tongues. "*All kinds of prayers and requests*" means what it says: we must pray in lots of different ways for lots of different things.

The passage does not say "pray sometimes," "pray intermittently," "pray only when you feel moved," or "pray only when you are in critical need." Paul says we must pray *always*. Pray, pray, pray. Prayer is to our life with God what breath is to life for our natural body. No breath, no life. No prayer, no life. And if we flip this concept, we can say that much prayer results in a supernatural life in God!

Because the kingdom of God covers a lot of territory, any one of us (or even any group of us) can pray for only a small portion of it in our lifetime. But without our prayers, old ground will be lost and new ground will not be gained. Taken together, our prayer efforts pay off in big ways with great advances.

The important thing for each of us is to pray prayers that strike the mark. With unlimited subject matter to pray for, we limited humans need to carefully choose not only our spiritual weapons and methods but also our targets. Of necessity, we must specialize, thus getting better at particular forms of prayer over time.

WHAT HAS GOD GIVEN YOU?

Our all-knowing God has no difficulty responding to prayers in all languages about all subjects, all prayed simultaneously. He wishes believers would pray more diverse prayers, while we continue to limit our prayers to one or two narrow categories, depending on what we are most familiar with. In this chapter, I want to open your eyes to (or provide a refresher on) different ways of looking at prayer. I want to explore the options so that you can find and focus on the kinds of prayer for which you are best equipped, and I want to challenge you to conquer new territory.

You have the most authority in prayer when you pray out of your own position in the body of Christ, the specific calling to which you have been assigned by God. In addition, the best way to grow in that calling is to give yourself to prayer that arises from what He has given you.

Therefore, take a moment to consider what God has given you. Is it a "heart" for missionaries, for a nation, for a particular individual? How has He equipped you to best pray? With the weapon of worship, with a prayer list, in rote fashion, or with prophetic insights? Where do you tend to pray the best? In a certain room, walking outside, alone, or with others? On your knees next to your bed or marching around like a soldier? When does it tend to happen? At a certain time of day or spontaneously, anytime? In a prayer room or outside on a prayer assignment?

Let me reemphasize that you have the most authority to give away what you have received from God. This makes it a priority to discover what He has equipped you for—all so that your prayers will strike the mark. Yes, so that they will hit the bull's-eye!

VARIETIES OF PRAYER ANOINTING

Where intercessory prayer is concerned, various believers have identified a number of orientations and inclinations—a wealth of valid variations of prayer. Like everything else in our experience of living in the Spirit, these categories can overlap and color each other. Yet highlighting them individually can be very useful as we explore our options.

Elizabeth (Beth) Alves, who is sometimes called "the grandma of the prayer shield," is one of those believers who has identified varieties of prayer anointing. I must give her credit for the twelve intercessor "specialties" that follow.[6] Beth is the founder of Increase International, a consultant to many ministry and business leaders, and a part of the Founders Group of the Apostolic Council of Prophetic Elders. We have walked together in prayer ministry for years—something I consider an honor.

1. GENERAL INTERCESSOR

General intercessors are prayer warriors who love to use prayer lists and never seem to get bored with them. I am not a "list intercessor" myself, but I am glad that many people are. General intercessors tend to be disciplined in their approach to prayer. They do not depend upon receiving a special unction or burden from the Holy Spirit before they engage in their assigned prayer task. They are good communicators, very pragmatic, and uncommonly dedicated.

General intercessors cover the waterfront in terms of their preferred prayer focus. Throughout the categories of intercessors that follow, you will always find general intercessors faithfully praying from their prayer lists. If you are a list intercessor, I say to you, "Go for it! And please add me to your list." I myself just cannot maintain this kind of praying for very long.

2. PERSONAL INTERCESSOR

Personal intercessors do not pray as much for projects, crises, or groups of people as they do for specific people. Their prayers may target the needs of only one person or of several people who may or may not be connected with each other. They bring a particular person by name before the Lord for a period of months or even years.

At different seasons of my life, I have been a personal intercessor for others who minister the gospel. Some of the prayer assignments have lasted a long time, such as my commitment to pray for Mahesh Chavda and his wife, Bonnie. Undoubtedly, my prayers are a vital part

---

6. For more detail about these categories and helpful reading about intercessory prayer, see Alves' books *Becoming a Prayer Warrior* (Grand Rapids, MI: Chosen Books, 2016) and *Intercessors: Discover Your Prayer Power*, written with Tommi Femrite and Karen Kaufman (Grand Rapids, MI: Chosen Books, 2000).

of the prayer support they need so that they can have such an effective ministry through their church in South Carolina, where miracles of healing have occurred over and over.

At times, you might be invited to become an individual's personal intercessor, but other times you might just decide to do so. For example, I prayed for Ché Ahn of Harvest International Ministry for seventeen years before I really got to know him. I happened to shake his hand at a conference in the late 1970s and a burden for prayer came upon me. I had not asked for it and I did not yet know Ché, but I was glad to pray. Over the years, the assignment became clearer as the magnitude of his ministry increased.

I am very grateful for my own personal intercessors. Who knows how many times their prayers have made a significant difference in my life and ministry?

3. FINANCIAL INTERCESSOR

Financial intercessors are sometimes known as "marketplace intercessors" because finances and the marketplace (business) are so intertwined. These believers have been given a gift of faith specifically for finances—for individuals, ministries, cities, and regions. They love to intercede for provision to be released for the work of the ministry or the prospering of a city or nation.

Money almost never falls from heaven, does it? Instead, people must work for it and share it. The prayers of financial intercessors release the provision that is needed for families and groups that minister to others.

You can see how these various kinds of prayer anointings overlap, because some financial intercessors also pray as personal intercessors or as one of the other prayer assignments described below.

4. CRISIS INTERCESSOR

I am a crisis intercessor—big-time. My prayers come alive when a crisis needs them, even if it comes in the middle of the night. Crisis intercessors pray for short-term, emergency situations, such as natural catastrophes, serious sicknesses, or wars. They are task-oriented by nature. Far from feeling put upon when called, crisis intercessors rise to the occasion, alert and fully engaged, even if they had been busy with something else or sleeping at the time.

Often enough, it has been my experience that God's Holy Spirit will alert me ahead of time to start praying for something major that is on the horizon. This comes from being a prophetic intercessor. I do not have to know all the details in order to pray effectively; I simply pray as the Spirit leads and until the burden lifts.

Rees Howells was a great crisis intercessor, and he taught others to pray too. His prayers were very effective. Among other things, he prayed hard during World War II to keep Nazi Germany from invading the United Kingdom, specifically Wales. You can read about him in Norman Grubb's book *Rees Howells, Intercessor*[7] and in my book *Prayer Storm*, where I devote an entire chapter to this strategic prayer assignment.[8]

5. SPIRITUAL WARFARE INTERCESSOR

Similar to crisis intercessors in many ways, spiritual warfare intercessors are not afraid to engage the devil's forces. Advancing on their knees "commando-style," they prevail against demonic strongholds. They often have the gift of discerning of spirits, and they specialize in strategic, on-location prayer. These prayer warriors have a focused goal in mind: they want to badger the devil and thwart his works of darkness in Jesus's great name.

Cindy Jacobs is a well-known prophetic intercessor who is both a crisis intercessor and, in particular, a spiritual warfare intercessor. She moves in a significant amount of spiritual authority to push back the darkness, and she is not afraid to step out where others will not go.

6. WORSHIP INTERCESSOR

Concerted praise and worship creates a holy flow that causes inspired intercession to pour forth from these priestly

7. Norman Grubb, *Rees Howells, Intercessor* (Fort Washington, PA: CLC Publications, 2016).
8. See footnote 4.

intercessors. Theirs is the kind of prayer that (because of the well-known International House of Prayer in Kansas City) we call today "harp and bowl," referring to this passage in the book of Revelation:

> *The four living creatures and the twenty-four elders fell down before the Lamb. Each one had a **harp** and they were holding golden **bowls** full of incense, which are the prayers of God's people.*
> (Revelation 5:8 NIV)

It goes without saying that all of us should be worship intercessors, but certain ones among us consider this style of prayer their primary calling. In fact, many contemporary worship lyrics are actual prayers, penned by worship intercessors and used as song-prayers. I have lived in the greater Nashville, Tennessee (Music City, U.S.A.), area for the past twenty years, so I know this category very well. Worshipping intercessors and interceding worshippers are everywhere there!

7. GOVERNMENTAL INTERCESSOR

All of us have a scriptural mandate to pray for those who exercise governmental authority over us. Paul's instructions to Timothy apply to each of us as well: *"I exhort first of all that supplications, prayers, intercessions, and giving of thanks be made for all men, for kings and all who are in authority, that we may lead a quiet and peaceable life in all godliness and reverence"* (1 Timothy 2:1–2). We should always pray by name for our president, prime minister, king or queen, or other current national figure who sits at the helm of our nation. We can extend this mandate to apply to lower-level governmental authorities. Sometimes we may become personal intercessors for them.

However, certain intercessors feel called to pray consistently, persistently, and enthusiastically for state, national, and international leaders, by name. They also tend to carry particular moral and legislative issues before the throne of grace, praying for restoration and reformation. They pray solo, and they band together in prayer networks. Intercessors for America is an especially enduring example of such a network. I could also highlight the ministry of Dutch Sheets, who exercises significant authority in governmental intercession.

Where I live in the state of Tennessee, the Tennessee Governmental Prayer Alliance keeps intercessors up-to-date about every piece of state legislation and political contest. The transmittal of that information is a vital part of the intercession effort and they do an exemplary job of it.

8. PEOPLE GROUP AND MISSIONS INTERCESSOR

These valuable prayer warriors have an unquenchable passion to pray for those who have not yet heard the gospel message. They may well specialize in their prayers. Some may pray mostly for Muslims or Buddhists or Hindus, while others may pray for people groups around the world that follow traditional, indigenous beliefs—as well as those who have no identifiable religion at all. Some may be personal intercessors for missionaries by name or for certain missions outreaches. Others may pray for refugees in times of war or for other people who come to their attention because they have been displaced from their homes.

Over the last few decades, it is such intercessors who have felt led to pray for those who live in the "10/40 window." (This is a way of designating the swathe of the globe that lies between the tenth and fortieth parallels, where the majority of the unreached Asian, Middle Eastern, and North African populations live. A number of these intercessors are also now praying for the "40/70 window"—an area in Europe and Asia north of the 10/40 window—to essentially reach people living in "post-Christian" cultures.) Many people group and missions intercessors pray from lists, but some pray primarily in crisis situations or when a special thrust or outreach has been planned.

9. SALVATION AND REVIVAL INTERCESSOR

Scripture passages about the salvation of the lost and laborers needed for the spiritual harvest are engraved on the hearts and minds of salvation and revival intercessors. (See, for example, Matthew 9:37–38; Luke 19:10; John 6:44; John 14:6; Romans 6:17; Romans 10:1, 14; Ephesians 6:19–20; 2 Peter 3:9; Ezekiel 11:19; Ezekiel 36:27.) They pray fervently for people to come to Christ, to give ear to Him, and to make a sustained commitment to Him. They pray for them to be filled with the Holy Spirit. They pray for more laborers for the harvest. They pray for those who tell the lost about Christ, often by name.

Salvation and revival intercessors make great personal backup people for those with outreach ministries. All successful evangelists have been backed up by at least one salvation and revival intercessor. You may remember the name of Charles Finney in conjunction with the Second Great Awakening in America, but few people realize that a man named Daniel "Father" Nash was his "secret weapon." Father Nash prayed for revival in city after city. Privately, he would go to a place prior to one of Finney's revival crusades and just pray. He would pray throughout the meetings as well. His prayers helped to prepare the spiritual soil of the region and people's hearts. About half a million converts are accorded to Finney's legacy, but Nash gave the assist on every single one of those personal decisions for Christ.

10. ISRAEL INTERCESSOR

Pray for the peace of Jerusalem: "May they prosper who love you." (Psalm 122:6)

Israel intercessors are watchmen and women who pray for the peace of Jerusalem, for the Middle East, and for God's purposes among the Jewish people worldwide. Their hearts weep over Jerusalem, as Jesus's did:

Jerusalem, Jerusalem, you who kill the prophets and stone those sent to you, how often I have longed to gather your children together, as a hen gathers her chicks under her wings, and you were not willing. (Matthew 23:37 NIV)

These intercessors band together with like-minded believers to pray. Their prayer focus does not mean that they do not pray for other countries, even those that are enemies of Israel, but they do it from their position as watchmen on the walls of Jerusalem.

The Caleb Company, founded by Don Finto and headquartered in Nashville, is a tremendous example of an intercessory group that focuses on Israel. Additional examples are Succat Hallel (Tabernacle of Praise) in Jerusalem, founded by Rick and Patti Ridings, and Jerusalem House of Prayer for All Nations on the Mount of Olives, founded by Tom Hess. More than ever, Israel prayer watches abound in our day.

I have also given much of my life to this particular arena, which has led to my leading prayer tours to Israel and other nations, as well as writing books such as *Praying for Israel's Destiny* and *The Coming Israel Awakening*.[9]

11. CHURCH AND LEADERSHIP INTERCESSOR

Church and leadership intercessors may also be personal intercessors, revival intercessors, financial intercessors, and more. (Most of us are actually "hyphenated" intercessors.) In Nashville, I helped start the Worship City Alliance, which monthly brings together leaders of congregations and ministries to seek the Lord in prayer together. This is an expression of church and leadership intercessors coming together for the common good.

I picture these valiant men and women as modern-day Aarons and Hurs who endeavor to lift up the arms of the Moseses of their generation. (See Exodus 17:8–13.) The hand of the Lord comes upon such intercessors, and their prayer burden involves their own portion of the body of Christ and its leaders. They pray for the unity and revival of the bride (the church) and for a hedge of protection to be raised up around the leaders of the community of believers with whom they are connected.

12. PROPHETIC INTERCESSOR

Prophetic intercessors pray with whatever particular focus the Holy Spirit gives them. They are the ones who listen and hear, look and see, and feel the burden of the Lord. The grace to pray like this combines the offices of prophet and priest in one person. The widow named Anna (see Luke 2:36–38) combined the power and passion of

9. *Praying for Israel's Destiny* (Grand Rapids, MI: Chosen Books, 2005); *The Coming Israel Awakening* (Grand Rapids, MI: Chosen Books, 2009).

prophetic intercession. Like Anna, prophetic intercessors long for the purposes of God to be birthed and come into full maturity in their generation. To that end, they are tireless in their prayers.

Instead of being agenda-oriented, these intercessors tend to be spontaneous, praying by the spirit of revelation. This is where the waters of God's purposes run deepest in my own life.[10]

ADDITIONAL EXPRESSIONS OF THE SPIRIT OF PRAYER

This chapter about the many faces of prayer would be incomplete without a discussion of forms and styles of prayer. Beyond our primary focus and subject matter, *how* do we pray? The answer may fall into one of these categories: contemplative forms of prayer, prayers with fasting, authoritative intercessory prayers, and deep prayers that are not in understandable language.

In *contemplative forms of prayer*, we wait in silence, watching and listening before God's throne to see what He may want to tell us. We do not keep track of the time or hurry the process. We consider our own spiritual standing before God, and we may need to pray penitent, cleansing prayers. We may read portions of Scripture slowly, savoring them and attending to His voice through them. Today, we use the term "soaking prayer and worship" to refer to this way of praying. It is my conviction that this is a modern-day expression of an age-old pattern that people used to call "waiting on the Lord."

At times, our contemplative prayer will be accompanied by *fasting*, or we may decide to fast for a stretch of time as we go about our ordinary activities. Fasting has a long history in Scripture and in the church, and it underlines and highlights our prayers. We might undertake a total fast from all meals for a predetermined length of time, or a partial fast in which we only omit certain types of food. Sometimes people decide to fast from something entirely removed from food, such as social media or the like.

---

10. For much more detail about prophetic intercessors, see my book *Praying with God's Heart: The Power and Purpose of Prophetic Intercession* (see footnote 2).

Occasions will arise for *authoritative intercessory prayers*—prayers that are declarative and even imperative rather than petitionary. This type of intercession is most useful in spiritual warfare or when overcoming intractable strongholds or difficulties. With help from the gifts of discerning of spirits and faith, we can step forward with confidence, even experiencing direct angelic assistance if necessary.

Not all prayers will be spoken in our native language. Sometimes we will pray *deep prayers that are not in understandable language*, or not even in words at all. Many times, we may pray (or sing) in tongues. We may groan or weep or wrestle or travail. This kind of Spirit-led praying is guaranteed to strike the mark every time:

> In the same way the Spirit also helps our weakness; for we do not know how to pray as we should, but the Spirit Himself intercedes for us with groanings too deep for words; and He who searches the hearts knows what the mind of the Spirit is, because He intercedes for the saints according to the will of God.
>
> (Romans 8:26–27 NASB)

MOVE WITH THE HEART OF GOD

I am amazed when I see how prayers that strike the mark take on many different faces, expressions, and anointings of the Holy Spirit depending on the circumstances. Please note that even if you start to feel you have it all figured out, your prayer expression will change from one season of your life to another. It is not just about getting answers to prayer. If Jesus remains at the center of all you do, you will continue to move with the very heart of God Himself.

None of us can pray in every way for everything. But together, we can do it. On this basis, we can confirm, with the apostle Paul, that we are all called to all prayers: *"with all prayer and supplication"* (Ephesians 6:18).

Let's get on board with it! It is always time to pray, all the time and in all different ways—all for the sake of God's great name. May His kingdom come on earth as it is in heaven!

TARGET PRACTICE

Gracious Father, in the wonderful name of Jesus, I thank You for Your Word, which is a lamp to my feet and a light to my path. Thank You for the clarity of instruction that is coming forth in our day and time. Release a greater empowerment of the Holy Spirit to every intercessor, an increase of the spirit of revelation to go with the specific assignments of each watchman on the wall. Grant to every one of us renewed focus and strength to keep on praying faithfully. Amen and amen! (See Psalm 119:105; Isaiah 62:6–7.)

4

REMINDING GOD OF
HIS WORD

*"Remember Your congregation, which You have purchased of old,
which You have redeemed to be the tribe of Your inheritance; and
this Mount Zion, where You have dwelt."*
—Psalm 74:2 (NASB)

Whether we know it or not, a spiritual war rages around us, and you and I have been chosen to participate in it as intercessors. The following passage is our invitation. I have underlined and highlighted these verses in my Bible, and you might wish to do so as well:

On your walls, O Jerusalem, I have appointed watchmen; all day and all night they will never keep silent. You who remind the LORD, take no rest for yourselves; and give Him no rest until He establishes and makes Jerusalem a praise in the earth.

(Isaiah 62:6–7 NASB)

Each of us has been appointed to a specific position on the "wall" from which we can watch and pray and sometimes fight for the sake of the kingdom of God. After having been divinely invited into God's presence, we have been assigned the tasks He has predetermined for us, by which we can do our part to help bring heaven to earth. Once more, at the most basic level, you have been appointed to the role of watchman over a certain portion of the kingdom wall, for a certain stretch of time.

What do we do on the wall? We watch and pray. And our prayer, according to this passage, entails "reminding" the Lord of His plan. As we observe things from our post, we tell Him what we see, ask Him what to do next, lean on His strength—and remind Him of how He has promised to take care of every situation.

WHAT WILL YOU REMIND HIM OF?

We are supposed to "give God no rest" as we remind Him. (See Isaiah 62:7.) That sounds difficult. How is it possible? How can we learn to do something like that?

First, the best way to pursue Him is to immerse ourselves in the written Word of God. Then we will know what to remind Him of. As part of our continual communication with Him, we can take His written Word as our guide—even down to the exact wording at times. The Bible is filled with promises God has made and a history of how He has handled things. When God's people have been in trouble, He has spoken to them. He is our Redeemer and His redemption is ongoing. He wants us to pursue Him so that we will know what to pray for—so that our prayers will strike the mark.

With the psalmist Asaph, we can cry out, "**Remember** *Your congregation, which You have purchased of old, the tribe of Your inheritance, which You have redeemed*" (Psalm 74:2). We can remind Him, "You are our Redeemer. We need You desperately." We can cry out on behalf of those who cannot cry out on their own.

We can remind God of His covenant with us and ask Him to uphold it despite our sinfulness. We can confess our own sins and the sins of the people we are connected with. We can plead the honor and glory of His name, reminding Him that He has said His glory will cover the earth as the waters cover the sea. (See Habakkuk 2:14.)

We can pray for healing and we can pray for mercy. If we begin to sound like the prophet Jeremiah in our desperation, so much the better:

LORD, have you completely rejected Judah? Do you really hate Jerusalem? Why have you wounded us past all hope of healing? We hoped for peace, but no peace came. We hoped for a time of healing, but found only terror. LORD, we confess our wickedness and that of our ancestors, too. We all have sinned against you. For the sake of your reputation, LORD, do not abandon us. Do not disgrace your own glorious throne. Please remember us, and do not break your covenant with us. Can any of the worthless foreign gods send us rain? Does it fall from the sky by itself? No, you are the one, O LORD our God! Only you can do such things. So we will wait for you to help us. (Jeremiah 14:19–22 NLT)

Remember, O LORD, what has befallen us; look, and see our reproach! Our inheritance has been turned over to strangers, our houses to aliens. We have become orphans without a father, our mothers are like widows. We have to pay for our drinking water, our wood comes to us at a price. Our pursuers are at our necks; we are worn out, there is no rest for us. (Lamentations 5:1–5 NASB)

As you can see, we can remind the Lord of His relationship with us and with His other children, essentially saying, "You are a Father who has pity on His children. So, I know You will hear my prayer!" We can plead with Him based on His attributes, such as lovingkindness, faithfulness, justice, and goodness.

In addition, we can cry out purely on the basis of the sorrows and needs of the people we are praying for, identifying with them as we do so. That may sound somewhat depressing, but it doesn't have to be. Yes, we intercessors can become weighed down with the sufferings of those we pray for, but this burden can be balanced out by remembering the all-sufficient God to whom we are speaking. By bearing the burdens of others to His throne, we can make a significant difference. (See Galatians 6:2.)

What else can we remind Him of? How about past answers to prayer? In many ways, this amounts to reminding ourselves too. It builds our faith. The more you remind Him of how He has helped you and others in the past, the more firmly you can stand before Him in expectation now. He can give you insights and revelation so that you can fine-tune your prayers to match His character, His heart, and His will.

You can pray, "You are the God who parted the Red Sea when the children of Israel were about to be captured by their enemies. When Moses stretched out his rod with authority, the sea was parted by Your powerful breath. Out of Zion salvation will come, and I am praying for salvation right now for _____." (See Psalm 14:7.)

You can pray, "Lord, You sent Your angels to deliver Peter from prison. Send angels now to help _____." (See Acts 12:1–19.)

You can plead the blood of Jesus on behalf of yourself and others. It would take another whole chapter to elaborate on this theme! Suffice it to say that it is all-important to pray on the basis of the efficacy of Jesus's blood to pay for sin, to cleanse and heal, and to bring new life.

As you recall other times of spiritual breakthrough, you can pray, "Your people need revival once again. Come again as You did before." Essentially, you testify about God's power and goodness as you remind Him, yourself, and the community of believers around you of what He is capable of doing. Others can add to your prayers, and their amens will make the prayers more effective.

As you plead the Word of God and the promises of God, you will find out what it means to pray under an anointing. The promises of God are "*yes*" and "*Amen*": "*For as many as are the promises of God, in Him they are yes; therefore also through Him is our Amen to the glory of God through us*" (2 Corinthians 1:20 NASB).

You can remind God of prayers you find in Scripture. Word-based prayers flow easily once you get underway. On your own, you might not be able to pray for more than five minutes, but with the Bible in front of you, you can remain at your station as a watchman on the wall indefinitely.

To assist you in selecting some helpful prayers from the Word, I have assembled scriptural prayers in the three Prayer Resources at the end of this book: "Prophetic Promises of Restoration," "Scriptural Prayers and Blessings," and "Prayers in the Psalms." I selected these prayers based on lists created by Mike Bickle of the International House of Prayer.

GOD'S WORD GIVES US GOD HIMSELF

The Word of God is absolutely essential to prayer. "Prayer may well be defined as the force that vitalizes and energizes the Word of God, by taking hold of God Himself," wrote intercessor and preacher E. M. Bounds in his book *The Necessity of Prayer*. He explained:

> The Word of God is the support upon which the lever of prayer is placed, and by which things are mightily moved. God has committed Himself, His purpose, and His promise to prayer. His Word becomes the basis and the inspiration of our praying. Under certain circumstances, persistent prayer may bring additional assurance of His promises. It is said of the old saints that they *"through faith…obtained promises"* (Hebrews 11:33). There would seem to be the capacity in prayer for going beyond the Word, beyond His promise, and into the very presence of God Himself.[11]

In his classic book *With Christ in the School of Prayer*, Andrew Murray quoted John 15:7—*"If ye abide in me, and my words abide in you, ye shall ask what ye will, and it shall be done unto you"* (KJV)—and then explained how abiding in Jesus is the same as abiding in His Word:

> The vital connection between the Word and prayer is one of the simplest and earliest lessons of the Christian life. As that newly converted heathen put it: "I pray—I speak to my

11. E. M. Bounds, *The Necessity of Prayer* (New Kensington, PA: Whitaker House, 1984), 115.

Father; I read—my Father speaks to me." Before prayer, God's Word strengthens me by giving my faith its justification and its petition. And after prayer, God's Word prepares me by revealing what the Father wants me to ask. In prayer, God's Word brings me the answer, for in it the Spirit allows me to hear the Father's voice....

It is this connection between His Word and our prayers that Jesus points to when He said, *"If ye abide in me, and my words abide in you, ye shall ask what ye will, and it shall be done unto you."* The deep importance of this truth becomes clear if we notice the expression that this one replaces. More than once Jesus had said, *"Abide in me, and I in you"* (John 15:4). His abiding in us was the complement and the crown of our abiding in Him. But here, instead of *"ye in me, and I in you"* (John 14:20), He said, *"Ye...in me, and my words...in you."* The abiding of His words is the equivalent of Himself abiding....

God, however, is the infinite Being in whom everything is life, power, spirit, and truth, in the very deepest meaning of the words. When God reveals Himself in His words, He does indeed give Himself—His love and His life, His will and His power—to those who receive these words, in a reality passing comprehension. In every promise, He gives us the power to grasp and possess Himself. In every command, He allows us to share His will, His holiness, and His perfection. God's Word gives us God Himself....

...In His words His will is revealed. As the words abide in me, His will rules me. My will becomes the empty vessel that His will fills and the willing instrument that His will rules.[12]

How vital the written Word of God is! It establishes an unbreakable connection between us and the Lord Himself and gives form and substance even to our most hidden prayers.

---

12. Andrew Murray, *With Christ in the School of Prayer* (New Kensington, PA: Whitaker House, 1981), 193–195, 199.

A MODERN-DAY EXAMPLE: DICK SIMMONS

My friend Dick Simmons has been one of my mentors for many years. Although most men his age would have retired by now, Dick continues to pray for hours every day. In 1970, he founded Men for Nations whereby men pray early in the morning at a location right on Capitol Hill in Washington, D.C., next to the Supreme Court. From 5:00 to 7:00 a.m., they combine their voices in Word-based prayer sessions on behalf of governmental leaders and the United States.

Prior to his work with Men for Nations, Dick, an ordained Presbyterian minister, played a key role in establishing the ministries of David Wilkerson and Pat Robertson, and he worked with significant justice-related initiatives.

Back in 1958, Dick was already an intercessor. One night, he was praying outdoors on the banks of the Hudson River, crying out to the Lord for New York City at the top of his voice, "Lord, I beseech Thee that You send forth laborers unto Your field!" (in the words of Matthew 9:37–38 and Luke 10:2). Here is what I wrote about this incident in my book *The Lost Art of Intercession*:

> His agonized prayers were so loud at 2:00 a.m. (even by New York City standards!) that he suddenly was bathed in floodlights on the riverbank. Cautious police officers shouted out, "What are you doing? You have been reported for disturbing the peace because you've been waking up people!"
>
> Dick bellowed back, "Oh, I am just praying to the Lord of the harvest that He would send forth laborers into His field."
>
> The police officers must have been shocked, or else they agreed with Brother Simmons. They let him go without any charges or warning. That very night, the Holy Spirit of God descended on a little skinny preacher in rural Pennsylvania and gave him a divine call to take the gospel to New York City. Do you know his name? It was David Wilkerson. It is no wonder that when Pastor Wilkerson established the first Teen

Challenge Center in New York City, he chose Dick Simmons to be its first director.[13]

I first met Dick in 1986 through our mutual friend Mahesh Chavda during a missions trip to Haiti. We have prayed together numerous times. Every time we do, we pray the Word, reminding the Lord of His promises. History proves how effective this kind of praying can be!

WISDOM, POWER, LOVE

As we learn to live as people of the Word, we are changed into God's likeness. This makes our prayers increasingly more effective. What does it mean to live as people of the Word? We gain glimpses of this lifestyle in the New Testament. For example, the apostle Paul praised the Colossians for the aspects of God's life that they displayed:

> *We always thank God, the Father of our Lord Jesus Christ, when we pray for you, because we have heard of your faith in Christ Jesus and of the love you have for all God's people—the faith and love that spring from the hope stored up for you in heaven and about which you have already heard in the true message of the gospel that has come to you. In the same way, the gospel is bearing fruit and growing throughout the whole world—just as it has been doing among you since the day you heard it and truly understood God's grace.… For this reason, since the day we heard about you, we have not stopped praying for you. We continually ask God to fill you with the knowledge of his will through all the wisdom and understanding that the Spirit gives, so that you may live a life worthy of the Lord and please him in every way: bearing fruit in every good work, growing in the knowledge of God, being strength-ened with all power according to his glorious might.*
> (Colossians 1:3–6, 9–11 NIV)

The gospel message alone is enough to make new men and women of us, let alone the written Word of God as we have it today in the New

---

13. James W. Goll, *The Lost Art of Intercession*, rev. and exp. ed. (Shippensburg, PA: Destiny Image, 2016), 150–151.

Testament. Having invited His Holy Spirit into our lives, we embark on a lifelong adventure of growing in liberty.

By God's wisdom, we learn to prayerfully administer His purposes in our little corner of the world. (See Ephesians 3:9–10.) Jesus promised to send His Spirit to be our Helper (see John 14:16, 26), and He is truly with us, keeping secure our connection with the Father so we can pray according to His will:

When the Spirit of truth comes, he will guide you into all truth. He will not speak on his own but will tell you what he has heard. He will tell you about the future. He will bring me glory by telling you whatever he receives from me. All that belongs to the Father is mine; this is why I said, "The Spirit will tell you whatever he receives from me."… Then you will ask in my name.
(John 16:13–15, 26 NLT)

The Spirit enables the church to operate in a spirit of revelation, corporately releasing God's power through our prayerful actions (see, for example, Acts 2) and even having authority over demons in Jesus's name (see, for example, Luke 9:1).

Clothed increasingly in God's holiness and other character qualities, we can aim our prayers with scriptural accuracy:

- We can pray for the conviction of sin, righteousness, and judgment. (See John 16:8.)

- We can pray for the release of the peace and joy of the Comforter in the fear of God. (See Acts 9:31; 2 Corinthians 1:3–4.)

- We can pray for true faith, trust, and hope. (See, for example, Romans 15:13.)

- We can pray for the power of the Word upon its hearers. (See, for example, Hebrews 4:12; Jeremiah 23:29; Acts 2:37–41.)

Do you grasp the significance of all this? With God's love in our hearts, His wisdom in our minds, and His Word to confirm His will, our prayers will strike the mark every time!

TARGET PRACTICE

In his book *With Christ in the School of Prayer*, Andrew Murray included the following petition, which, as watchmen on the wall, we can make our own:

> Blessed Lord, I see why my prayer has not been more believing and effective. I was more occupied with my speaking to You than with Your speaking to me. I did not understand that the secret of faith is this: there can be only as much faith as there is of the living Word dwelling in the soul.
>
> Your Word taught me so clearly to be *"swift to hear"* and *"slow to speak"* (James 1:19), and not to be hasty to say just anything to God. Lord, teach me that it is only when I take Your Word into my life that my words can be taken into Your heart. Teach me that if Your Word is a living power within me, it will be a living power with You, also. Show me that what Your mouth has spoken Your hand will perform.
>
> Lord Jesus,…give me the opened ear of the learner, wakened morning by morning to hear the Father's voice. Just as You speak only what You hear from the Father, may my speaking be the echo of Your speaking to me. *"When Moses was gone into the tabernacle…to speak with him, then he heard the voice of one speaking unto him from off the mercy seat"* (Numbers 7:89). Lord, may it be so with me, too. Let my life and character reveal that Your words abide and are seen in me. May this be my preparation for the complete blessing: *"Ye shall ask what ye will, and it shall be done unto you."* Amen.[14] (See 2 Chronicles 6:15; Isaiah 50:4–5; John 12:49.)

---

14. Murray, *With Christ*, 200–201.

5

REMOVING THE OBSTACLES

"Those from among you will rebuild the ancient ruins;
you will raise up the age-old foundations;
and you will be called the repairer of the breach,
the restorer of the streets in which to dwell."
—Isaiah 58:12 (NASB)

As we move forward as intercessors, we will inevitably encounter obstacles. It is a guaranteed part of our lives as followers of Jesus. The Lord Himself warned us about this in so many words: *"In this world you will have trouble"* (John 16:33 NIV). And He set the example for us: *"To this you were called, because Christ suffered for you, leaving you an example, that you should follow in his steps"* (1 Peter 2:21 NIV). The life of a disciple is challenging—and all the more if you set yourself against the powers of darkness as a watchman on the walls!

Many of these obstacles appear as hindrances, constraints, or weaknesses in our personal lives. *Baggage* might be the most useful term. We cannot move forward freely unless we get rid of our "stuff," which, one way or another, always has to do with sin. As we journey along and encounter such obstacles, we must identify them and seek God's perspective about them. It will not serve any good purpose to hide them (or hide behind them) or pick them up and try to keep carrying them.

ISAIAH'S ADMONITION

Fulfilling our God-given destiny depends upon our taking the words of Isaiah personally and seriously. He spoke about clearing out the obstacles that trip us up or block us: *"And it will be said, 'Build up, build up, prepare the way, remove every obstacle out of the way of My people'"* (Isaiah 57:14 NASB). As if that were not enough, he added this admonition: *"Go through, go through the gates, clear the way for the people; build up, build up the highway, remove the stones, lift up a standard over the peoples"* (Isaiah 62:10 NASB).

Again, in Isaiah 58, we are given a specific calling and purpose: *"Those from among you will rebuild the ancient ruins; you will raise up the age-old foundations; and you will be called the repairer of the breach, the restorer of the streets in which to dwell"* (verse 12 NASB). We are called not only to remove obstacles, but also to restore the moral standards of society. Cleaning up the mess is not the ultimate call—restoration is! We first remove the hindrances and then we rebuild, repair, and restore the "streets."

Don't you think the "streets" need some restoration in our time? On the Day of Atonement (Yom Kippur) a couple of years ago, I was given repeated dreams about God's heart concerning the condition of the major cities of North America. The dreams took me on a tour where I saw horrific urban blight. The scenes reminded me of a war zone, with bombed-out buildings everywhere. But then the voice of the Lord came to me, saying, "Everywhere there is desolation, there will be restoration. Everywhere there is devastation, there will be transformation."

This will come only as the people of God allow Him to bring light to their personal darkness so that they can undertake—largely through their prayers—the restoration of the society around them.

ONE AT A TIME

Years ago, while I was teaching a class, I read this verse aloud: *"For the earth will be filled with the knowledge of the glory of the LORD as the waters cover the sea*" (Habakkuk 2:14 NIV). It occurred to me that I did not really understand those words, so I mused aloud in front of the students, "How is the glory of the Lord going to cover the earth? How does that happen?"

Immediately, the Holy Spirit responded, "One clay pot at a time." In other words, as disciples of the Lord Jesus Christ, each one of us must be filled with the glory of God. If, one by one, we all become filled to overflowing with the glory realm of God, then eventually a neighborhood, a city, or a region could become saturated with God's goodness.

Yes, we need to repair the breaches and rebuild the cracked foundations in our own lives and families as part of the preliminary process of being empowered to effectively help others in the restorative and transformational calling regarding our cities. What obstacles of sin are you aware of in your own life? How can you remove them so that the way ahead of you is cleared? Is there a pattern revealed in the above Scriptures with which to line up your life? I think so.

We must address each sin-obstacle we run into. This is the only way we can clear the obstacles and become "repairers of the breach." This is the only way to move ahead in praying prayers that strike the mark. Just think about it: flailing around on your life journey will only cause you to produce prayers that *miss* the mark!

It is as the psalmist portrays it:

If I had cherished sin in my heart, the LORD would not have listened; but God has surely listened and has heard my prayer. Praise be to God, who has not rejected my prayer or withheld his love from me! (Psalm 66:18–20 NIV)

And the proverb-writer agrees: "*The LORD detests the sacrifice of the wicked, but he delights in the prayers of the upright*" (Proverbs 15:8 NLT).

I want to be upright, not wicked. Don't you? How can we turn things around and make sure that we stay on track with God? Where do we start? How do we begin the process?

THE FREEDOM OF CONFESSION

There is only one way to remove a sin-obstacle: confession and repentance. This assumes you understand what your "sin" is. Naturally, I am not talking only about murder and lying and stealing. Much of our sin is simple idolatry—holding a person, a concept, or an object in higher esteem than we hold God Himself. We find that generational repercussions follow unrepented idolatry:

> I am the LORD your God who brought you out of the land of Egypt, out of the house of slavery. You shall have no other gods before Me. You shall not make for yourself an idol, or any likeness of what is in heaven above or on the earth beneath or in the water under the earth. You shall not worship them or serve them; for I, the LORD your God, am a jealous God, visiting the iniquity of the fathers on the children, and on the third and the fourth generations of those who hate Me, but showing lovingkindness to thousands, to those who love Me and keep My commandments.
>
> (Deuteronomy 5:6–10 NASB)

Identifying the sin is half of the solution, because it helps you know what you are dealing with. Instead of being baffled by the things you have trouble with ("Why do I always get so upset when I face this person/situation?"), you can give them a name (pride, fear, jealousy). Thus enlightened, with the help of the Word of God, you can go on to the next step. Without looking into the mirror of the righteous standards of the Word of God, you can never understand right from wrong from God's point of view.

After you identify a sin, you must do something with that information—you need to move on to repentance and confession. How you approach confession may depend on your church affiliation and your background, but the outcome should be the same. First, before God, you state unequivocally how you have sinned. Then, you declare your intention—with God's help—to sin no more. Confession means admitting that you are guilty of something that you have been accused of or that you feel convicted of. You may acknowledge this guilt or conviction only to yourself and God, or you may tell a pastor, priest, or another godly individual. If you are confessing in the presence of another, that person may be able to prescribe helpful measures for you to take once you step back into your daily life.

Ultimately, though, it is not just about your confession or agreement. It is about the power of the shed blood of Jesus Christ to cleanse you from your sin. As the old gospel song states, "There is power, power, wonder-working power in the precious blood of the Lamb"! Scriptural confession leads to biblical cleansing. As another beloved hymn says, "What can wash away my sin? Nothing but the blood of Jesus."[15]

THE POWER OF FORGIVENESS

Many of us underestimate the power of God's forgiveness and therefore take it too lightly. Having been spared the consequences of our sin by our confession and repentance, we do not fully recognize what we have been saved from or how impossible our situation would be without God's grace. Even less do we recognize how powerful it can be to extend our forgiveness to others.

God's forgiveness does more than bring peace to our hearts—it breaks down walls and it turns on the light. In his book *The House of the Lord*, Francis Frangipane elaborated on the amazing power of God's forgiveness: "Forgiveness is the very spirit of heaven removing the hiding places of demonic activity from the caverns of the human soul. It is every wrong made right and every evil redeemed for good. The power released in forgiveness is actually a mighty weapon."[16] It really is, and I can testify to its power.

Forgiveness neutralizes bitterness and enmity. God-initiated forgiveness introduces His love into a loveless situation, and along with His love comes healing and deliverance—for all of the parties who were entangled in the sin.

---

15. See Lewis E. Jones, "There Is Power in the Blood," 1899; Robert Lowry, "What Can Wash Away My Sin?" 1876.
16. Francis Frangipane, *The House of the Lord* (Lake Mary, FL: Charisma House, 1996), 62.

Forgiveness is such a powerful weapon in spiritual warfare that Satan does everything he can to make us forget about it. He is known as "the accuser of the brethren" (see Revelation 12:10), and he will often accuse us of not having "done forgiveness right" or not having received enough forgiveness to do any good. It is true that our emotions often lag behind our actions. We might pray for God's forgiveness or extend forgiveness to another person, only to wonder if anything happened at all.

Do not try to figure it out on your own. Run to the Word of God and turn to your Father in heaven. Seek His encouragement and reassurance. Humbly admit that your sin nature is pervasive and persistent. Confess and repent again if you need to (and/or forgive again the person who has sinned against you). Where sin is concerned, "wash, rinse, repeat" is always good advice for any of us. That is why Christians talk about forgiveness so much, Sunday after Sunday in our worship services and many, many times in between. Open your New Testament almost anywhere and you will find another testimony to the power of forgiveness.

SHINE THE LIGHT OF THE WORD

Light and darkness—there is never a real contest between them. Flip on the switch of God's Word in your house and it will be filled with radiant light. The darkness will be displaced. Where does the darkness go? I don't know. It just flees!

So, hold on to your hat while I get a little liturgical on you. Remember, there are gems of truth hidden away in every major church tradition. To help turn on the light, I wanted to find a good collection of Scriptures about confession and repentance. I found it in the *Book of Common Prayer*, which has been used since 1549 (with some revisions) by the Anglican communion of churches, including the Episcopal Church in the United States. It is quite a list. The following are some of the Scriptures included. I have kept these verses in the King James Version for consistency:

When the wicked man turneth away from his wickedness that he hath committed, and doeth that which is lawful and right, he shall save his soul alive. (Ezekiel 18:27)

I acknowledge my transgressions: and my sin is ever before me. (Psalm 51:3)

Hide thy face from my sins, and blot out all mine iniquities. (Psalm 51:9)

The sacrifices of God are a broken spirit: a broken and a contrite heart, O God, thou wilt not despise. (Psalm 51:17)

Rend your heart, and not your garments, and turn unto the LORD *your God: for he is gracious and merciful, slow to anger, and of great kindness....* (Joel 2:13)

To the Lord our God belong mercies and forgivenesses, though we have rebelled against him; neither have we obeyed the voice of the LORD *our God, to walk in his laws, which he set before us by his servants the prophets.* (Daniel 9:9–10)

O LORD, *correct me, but with judgment; not in thine anger, lest thou bring me to nothing.* (Jeremiah 10:24; see also Psalm 6:1)

Repent ye: for the kingdom of heaven is at hand. (Matthew 3:2)

I will arise and go to my father, and will say unto him, Father, I have sinned against heaven, and before thee, and am no more worthy to be called thy son: make me as one of thy hired servants. (Luke 15:18–19)

Enter not into judgment with thy servant: for in thy sight shall no man living be justified. (Psalm 143:2)

If we say that we have no sin, we deceive ourselves, and the truth is not in us. If we confess our sins, he is faithful and just to forgive us our sins, and to cleanse us from all unrighteousness.

(1 John 1:8–9)

After laying a foundation of Scriptures such as these, the *Book of Common Prayer* goes on to include exhortations about removing obstacles of sin and specific prayers of confession. (These readings may be familiar to some people and new to others. I present them here simply as a good way to sum up what confession involves and to furnish a way to express it.)

The Minister shall say,

Dearly beloved brethren, the Scripture moveth us in sundry places to acknowledge and confess our manifold sins and wickedness; and that we should not dissemble nor cloak them before the face of Almighty God our heavenly Father; but confess them with an humble, lowly, penitent, and obedient heart; to the end that we may obtain forgiveness of the same, by his infinite goodness and mercy. And although we ought at all times humbly acknowledge our sins before God; yet ought we most chiefly so to do, when we assemble and meet together to render thanks for the great benefits that we have received at his hands, to set forth his most worthy praise, to hear his most holy Word, and to ask those things which are requisite and necessary, as well for the body as the soul. Wherefore I pray and beseech you, as many as are here present, to accompany me with a pure heart, and humble voice, unto the throne of the heavenly grace, saying—

A General Confession. *To be said by the whole Congregation, after the Minister, all kneeling.*

Almighty and most merciful Father, we have erred, and strayed from thy ways like lost sheep. We have followed too much the devices and desires of our own hearts. We have offended against thy holy laws. We have left undone those things which we ought to have done; and we have done those things which we ought not to have done; and there is no health in us. But thou, O Lord, have mercy upon us, miserable offenders. Spare thou those, O God, who confess their faults. Restore thou those that are penitent; according to thy promises declared unto mankind in Christ Jesus our Lord. And grant, O most merciful Father, for his sake; that we may hereafter live a godly, righteous, and sober life, to the glory of thy holy name. Amen.

(This normally is followed by the Prayer of Absolution or Remission of Sins, spoken by the Minister.)[17]

A CORPORATE CRY

By confessing our sins often and freely, we come into alignment not only with God's assessment of our sinful condition, but also with its cure, which is the blood of Jesus Christ. Additionally, this is how we can come into alignment with God on behalf of others in what many people call "identificational repentance" or "confessing generational sin." That is what Daniel did when he prayed, *"Alas, O Lord,…we have sinned, committed iniquity, acted wickedly and rebelled, even turning aside from Your commandments and ordinances"* (Daniel 9:4–5 NASB). His intercession opened the way for the fulfillment of the prophecy regarding the Israelites' return to their homeland. (See Jeremiah 25:1–14; 29:1–14.) It also helped to break the influence of the demonic principalities that had led the Hebrew people to abandon their worship of the one true God, resulting in their being taken into captivity in Babylon for seventy years in the judgment of God.

By pursuing the Lord and His ways, we come to understand the application for us today. God wants to bring cleansing and wholeness to the body of Christ, removing the "legal" grounds by which evil powers subject us to bondage. (I will go into more depth about this topic in the next chapter, "Exposing Demonic Gateways.")

---

17. *The Book of Common Prayer* (New York: Church Hymnal Corporation, 1943), 5–6.

In truth, demonic spirits have no true authority to exert their influence without some kind of permission. Such "permission" almost always takes the form of sin, either personal or corporate. Sin allows demonic spirits to set up camp and to spread oppression. Another way of saying this is that sin enables curses to take root and grow, producing much rotten fruit, such as mental and emotional breakdowns, chronic illnesses, frequent accidents, relational alienation and strife, poverty, and unnatural death.

I am sure you can see the connection: tackling issues of sin head-on makes effective intercession possible. Our initial task is to clear out the sin-obstacles from our own hearts and lives. Only after clearing out our own obstacles can we consider interceding for the needs of others, even whole nations, by doing our part to help eliminate their corporate sin-obstacles. Corporate sin-obstacles are the accumulated group sins that perpetuate all of the disorder and distress that we intercessors find ourselves so ready and willing to pray for.

What kinds of sins compel our corporate cry of, "Mercy, Lord!"? I will introduce this theme now and expand on it in the next chapter. Here is a basic list and some representative verses:

+ Idolatry. (See Exodus 20:1–5; Deuteronomy 7:5, 25–26; 1 Corinthians 10:19–20.)

+ Murder. (See Genesis 9:6; Exodus 20:13; Leviticus 17:11, 14; Numbers 35:33.)

+ Witchcraft and substance abuse. (See Leviticus 20:6; Revelation 17–18, 21:8.)

+ Adultery, sodomy, perversion, and other sexual sins. (See Leviticus 18 and 20:10–21; Deuteronomy 23:17; Romans 1:24–28; 1 Corinthians 5:1.)

+ Fighting, anger, hatred, cursing, and unforgiveness. (See Proverbs 17:13; Matthew 18:21–35; James 4:1–12.)

+ Rebellion against those in authority. (See Exodus 20:12; Leviticus 20:9; Hebrews 13:17; 1 Peter 2:13–20.)

Like Daniel, we need to shoulder the blame for our own contribution (even our silent assent or bitter judgment) to the sin of the group. We must "own" the sin enough to surrender it to God in a meaningful way, asking Him for His mercy and help. We may break curses or engage in other kinds of spiritual warfare—but only after demolishing the obstacles, which would be an impossibly monumental undertaking without God's grace every step of the way.[18]

FORGIVENESS AND FAITH

It is all about removing obstacles—first the sin in our own hearts, which blocks our forward progress along the road of righteousness and keeps us from praying aright, and then in the world around us, where the wreckage of sin is piled so high it blocks the sun.

All of this confession and repentance would be a worthless exercise if we did not have Jesus's forgiveness, which wipes our slate clean of sin and sets us back on our feet so that we can operate out of righteous faith: *"If we confess our sins, He is faithful and righteous to forgive us our sins and to cleanse us from all unrighteousness"* (1 John 1:9 NASB). No longer must we stumble along by our own light; we have the true light of Christ to show us the way. And through our intercessory prayers, we can draw others along with us on God's path as we pray, "Thy kingdom come, Thy will be done, on earth as it is in heaven."

By the way, did you know that the model prayer of Jesus known to us as the Lord's Prayer is not intended to be prayed on a purely individual basis? Take a look at the wording. The pronouns are plural; they include others repeatedly: *"Our Father...give us this day our daily bread...forgive us our sins as we forgive those who sin against us."*[19]

In other words, the prayer of Jesus is not meant to be used in personal devotions alone. It calls us to united, corporate prayer that causes intercessors to identify with the needs of family members, fellow citizens, and strangers. Jesus calls us not only to confess our

---

18. Much more on this topic can be learned from my book *Deliverance from Darkness* (Grand Rapids, MI: Chosen Books, 2010).
19. Jesus's prayer is found in Matthew 6:9–13 and Luke 11:2–4.

individual sins, but also to step into the gap and lift up intercessory pleas on behalf of others who cannot pray for themselves or who need extra prayer—confessing corporate faults, failures, and sins.

Let's keep up the good work, removing the sin-obstacles one after another as we encounter them so that we can proceed on our journey of faith, interceding as God leads and accurately striking the mark over and over with our prayers.

TARGET PRACTICE

Heavenly Father, I revere Your name above all others. I exalt Your sovereign lordship over my temporal circumstances and I choose to believe that the entrance of the light of Your Word brings conviction, truth, and revelation. Shine Your Word into my heart, dear Jesus! I declare the truth that as Your Word takes up new levels of residence in my heart, it displaces old levels of darkness. I proclaim that sin is being forgiven and the stain of guilt is being cleansed away. Obstacles are being removed and restoration is well underway. In the great name of Jesus, amen. (See Psalm 119:130.)

6

EXPOSING
DEMONIC GATEWAYS

*"For I do not want you to be ignorant of the fact, brothers and
sisters, that our ancestors were all under the cloud and that they
all passed through the sea. They were all baptized into Moses
in the cloud and in the sea. They all ate the same spiritual
food and drank the same spiritual drink; for they drank from
the spiritual rock that accompanied them, and that rock was
Christ. Nevertheless, God was not pleased with most of them;
their bodies were scattered in the wilderness. Now these things
occurred as examples to keep us from setting our hearts on evil
things as they did. Do not be idolaters, as some of them were; as
it is written: 'The people sat down to eat and drink and got up to
indulge in revelry.' We should not commit sexual immorality, as
some of them did—and in one day twenty-three thousand of them
died. We should not test Christ, as some of them did—and were
killed by snakes. And do not grumble, as some of them did—and
were killed by the destroying angel. These things happened to
them as examples and were written down as warnings for us, on
whom the culmination of the ages has come. So, if you think you
are standing firm, be careful that you don't fall!"*
—1 Corinthians 10:1–12 (NIV)

Even when we can identify the sin-obstacles that interfere with
our walk with the Lord, we may forget who or what is behind every

one—the tempter who lured Adam to sin so long ago. Today, sad to say, it appears that the enemy's fingerprints are on just about everything. We are so accustomed to them that we allow him to carry on his dirty work unchallenged.

Well, not forever. When intercessors get involved, they challenge the powers of darkness. People who know how to pray effectively also know how to apply the Word of God to figure out what, exactly, they are dealing with. They know that God's people have an enemy who opposes them at every opportunity. They also know that their prayers put a restraining order on the devil and the work of his demons. These warrior intercessors know how to enforce the victory of Calvary. At times, they even call on a reconnaissance force of angels to combat the temporary present darkness and to speak forth strategies that will release revival breakthrough.

The big picture is that the earth belongs to God, not to the enemy, and that the Lord has given stewardship over it to his delegated authority—"the sons of men," His people. (See, for example, Genesis 1:26; Matthew 28:18–20.) The more we can learn about how to exercise that authority, the better.

VIOLATIONS

Those who live by God's truth repent of their sins quickly, and the enemy cannot infiltrate their affairs. But violations of God's standards open the gates to the darkness. Needless to say, sin is prevalent in this world. Many people are busy sinning most of the time. They disregard or are ignorant of the Word of God and its Author. They see no reason to stop living in whatever way they want to. As a result, formidable sinful structures become established and the influence of darkness tends to prevail.

We call the enemy of God "the devil" or "Satan." He is a fallen angel, and we know that he spreads his dark influence by means of hordes of other dark angels known as demons. (See, for example, Revelation 12:9.) The last thing we want to do is to participate in their evil work. (See 1 Corinthians 10:20.) That is why we must pay attention to all of the warnings and instructions in Scripture—in both the Old and New Testaments—so that we can be fully aware of what is going on around us.

In the previous chapter, I listed some of the top reasons for enemy infiltration of people's lives. Now I want to devote a whole chapter to exposing such demonic entry points so that those of you in the body of Christ who stand in the gap and intercede for God's work can be informed as completely as possible. You could call this "informed intercession."

Please keep this fact in mind: demonic spirits have no true authority to influence anything without "legal" permission. The presence of certain sinful conditions gives them the authority to set up a base of operations from which to exercise oppression. Some of these sinful conditions are as follows. (Note: this is not an exhaustive list, and the entry points are not in any particular order.)

IDOLATRY

The sin of idolatry covers a lot more than worshipping little statues. Remember what Samuel said to sinful Saul, who had arrogantly disobeyed God's command:

> Has the LORD as much delight in burnt offerings and sacrifices as in obeying the voice of the LORD? Behold, to obey is better than sacrifice, and to heed than the fat of rams. For rebellion is as the sin of divination, and insubordination is as iniquity and idolatry. Because you have rejected the word of the LORD, He has also rejected you from being king.   (1 Samuel 15:22–23 NASB)

Saul had not worshipped a pagan image, but he had followed his own will rather than God's, something that every one of us is likely to do at times. Rebellion and insubordination equal idolatry. No amount of backpedaling and excuse-making on Saul's part could change that fact. (See 1 Samuel 15:10–29.) As a result, the evil one had a legal right to make his next move.

Truth be told, much of our typical behavior can be called idolatry, can't it? That may be why God put the prohibition against idolatry first when He gave His people the Ten Commandments:

> *I am the LORD your God, who rescued you from the land of Egypt, the place of your slavery. You must not have any other god but me. You must not make for yourself an idol of any kind or an image of anything in the heavens or on the earth or in the sea. You must not bow down to them or worship them, for I, the LORD your God, am a jealous God who will not tolerate your affection for any other gods. I lay the sins of the parents upon their children; the entire family is affected—even children in the third and fourth genera-tions of those who reject me.*   (Exodus 20:1–5 NLT)

Idolatry sounds serious because it is.

What do you do when you discover that you have already set up an idol in your life? You sincerely repent. You do not just feel sorry for a while about what you have done, but you turn around and stop sinning altogether. You take the advice of Moses to heart:

> *You must burn [the] idols in fire, and you must not covet the silver or gold that covers them. You must not take it or it will become a trap to you, for it is detestable to the LORD your God. Do not bring any detestable objects into your home, for then you will be destroyed, just like them. You must utterly detest such things, for they are set apart for destruction.* (Deuteronomy 7:25–26 NLT)

Today, very rarely do we need to take these words about burning our idols literally, because most of our idols are intangible, not physical objects that can be burned. But a good housecleaning is a smart thing to do. Once, after an intense and powerful time of ministry in Haiti, I discerned that what I call a "trailing spirit" had followed me home. But what was the basis of its right to operate in my home? I remembered I had purchased a handcrafted, wooden artifact as a souvenir. When I got rid of that object, I eliminated the enemy's counterattack, with its dark, heavy cloud of oppression. Out with the cursed object, out with the oppression.

In the Western world, our idols are more likely to consist of our bowing down to gold and silver (greed or mammon)—or just about anything else that we consult first, before God, regarding our lives. Once we recognize our idolatry, we must flat-out turn from our idols as completely as if we had incinerated them. Without a backward glance, we must run to our heavenly Father.

TEMPLES TO PAGAN RELIGIONS

This might seem to be another form of idolatry that no longer applies to us in the twenty-first century—until we look around and notice how many non-Christian houses of worship have been established in our cities: mosques, shrines, and other gathering places for devotees of various religions. In biblical times, one of the major violations of God's law was the establishment of "high places" of occult worship.[20] High places are not just physical locations. They are places of demonic activity and control—and these demonic forces have not vanished with the centuries. Although they are not much advertised, high places are still with us today. All such places, including Masonic lodges,[21] serve as open invitations to demonic forces.

We must walk in love toward all people, regardless of their religious convictions, but we must also walk watchfully, without blinders. It is a fact: pagan houses of worship give entrance to evil powers, and you may have to deal with the consequences as you engage in intercession.

MURDER AND THE SHEDDING OF INNOCENT BLOOD

"Thou shalt not kill" (Exodus 20:13; Deuteronomy 5:17 KJV)—the sixth commandment would seem to be as clear as it can be. Do not go around murdering or shooting other people. But with the exaltation of the "zombie death culture" in our society, things are not as clear to people as they were even fifty years ago. Moreover, with the help of

---

20. See, for example, Numbers 33:52; 2 Kings 17:11; 18:4; Psalm 78:58; Jeremiah 19:5; 32:35.
21. For more information, see Ron G. Campbell, *Free from Freemasonry* (Grand Rapids, MI: Baker Publishing Group, 1999); Cindy Jacobs, *Deliver Us from Evil* (Ventura, CA: Regal Books, 2001); and Caryl Matrisciana, *Gods of the New Age* (Irvine, CA: Harvest House, 1985).

the evil one, humankind has found any number of sly ways to murder innocent people, such as abortion and euthanasia. And with each murder always comes repercussions:

> *Whoever sheds man's blood, by man his blood shall be shed; for in the image of God He made man.*　　　　　(Genesis 9:6)

> *The life of all flesh is its blood.*　　　　　(Leviticus 17:14)

God gives value to life, every life. That is why He set it up so that when you break any of the Ten Commandments, they break you. To atone for the sin of shedding the blood of another person, more blood is required:

> *For the life of the flesh is in the blood, and I have given it to you upon the altar* [the blood of pure animals, prefiguring the blood of Jesus] *to make atonement for your souls; for it is the blood that makes atonement for the soul.*　　　　　(Leviticus 17:11)

> *So you shall not pollute the land where you are; for blood defiles the land, and no atonement can be made for the land, for the blood that is shed on it, except by the blood of him who shed it.*
> 　　　　　(Numbers 35:33)

The above ancient words lay out the sin of bloodshed and its consequences, and they do not offer much hope. But as we know now, the blood of Jesus atones for murder and all other violations of God's laws, for all time (although the murderer may still face punishment by the state). The trouble is, as intercessors, we too often do not discern what we are dealing with when we pray for our society. We may be interceding for our nation, our church, or our family. But unless we take hidden sins such as bloodshed or other forms of violence into account, we may fail to vanquish the enemy strongholds that have been refortified over many years.

Under the guise of "the right of compassionate death," "medically assisted dying," or "death with dignity," euthanasia and/or strictly regulated assisted suicide have been made legal in several nations and states of the United States. Abortion has been legal in the United States since 1973 and is legal in some form in almost 90 percent of the world's nations. And that is not all. Random public shootings and acts of terrorism are causing instances of violent death to mount.

As intercessors, we must recognize the culture of death that surrounds us and pray against it with our weapons of spiritual warfare.

WITCHCRAFT AND SUBSTANCE ABUSE

In certain parts of the world, witchcraft and neopagan worship are the fastest-growing religions. In Great Britain, for example, where religious affiliation can now be specified on census forms, upward of sixty thousand individuals identified as Wiccan, Pagan, or related categories in 2011.[22]

I place substance abuse in the witchcraft category because much alcohol and drug abuse (and the like), which often leads to addiction, is little more than witchcraft under a deceptive disguise of "fun." Both represent willfulness and rebellion and both open the gateway to serious demonic oppression. Remember Samuel's words to Saul: *"For rebellion is as the sin of divination, and insubordination is as iniquity and idolatry"* (1 Samuel 15:23 NASB).

By "witchcraft," I mean purposeful worship of a deity other than the Hebrew or Christian God. Witchcraft, in all of its forms, glorifies the dark side of the spiritual world, with special interest in knowing and controlling the future by means of a spiritual power source other than the true God. The Bible has a lot to say about witchcraft, using key words such as *sorcery, medium, divination,* and *necromancy* (consulting the dead). Before they entered the promised land, the people of Israel were warned not to adopt the pagan practices they would encounter:

When you enter the land the LORD your God is giving you, do not learn to imitate the detestable ways of the nations there. Let no one

22. "It's a Moot Point, but Paganism May Be the Fastest Growing Religion in Britain," *Yorkshire Post*, 31 October 2013, https://www.yorkshirepost.co.uk/news/analysis/it-s-a-moot-point-but-paganism-may-be-the-fastest-growing-religion-in-britain-1-6199786; Office for National Statistics, Census 2011, Religion, https://www.nomisweb.co.uk/census/2011/qs210ew.

be found among you who sacrifices their son or daughter in the fire, who practices divination or sorcery, interprets omens, engages in witchcraft, or casts spells, or who is a medium or spiritist or who consults the dead. Anyone who does these things is detestable to the Lord. (Deuteronomy 18:9–12 niv)

Under the law of Moses, the penalty for practicing witchcraft was physical (and spiritual) death. (See, for example, Exodus 22:18; Leviticus 20:27.) Under the new covenant, unless those who practice witchcraft repent, they will ultimately experience spiritual death as well. (See Revelation 17–18; 21:8.)

THE REMOVAL OF CHRISTIANITY FROM EDUCATIONAL INSTITUTIONS

In the name of "separation of church and state," the Christian viewpoint, prayer, and Bible reading have been eliminated from public educational institutions in the United States, starting in the 1950s. Consequently, moral and behavioral restraints have deteriorated as secular humanism has filled the void. When educators model to their students a human-centered, self-sufficient lifestyle devoid of reliance on faith, the evil one can declare open season.

The Scriptures portray the opposite approach, namely, teaching children to understand the world from a God-centered point of view. (See, for example, Exodus 12:26–28; Deuteronomy 4:9; 6:5–7; Ephesians 6:4.) Parents must take responsibility to teach their children the Word of God and the importance of prayer, and to model moral character. Many of the problems with our children arise when we implicitly transfer all of our parental authority to government-run public schools. The way that the family and the church have abdicated their roles and left it to the educational system to instill boundaries in children has not borne good fruit. It is past time for the institutions of family and church to repent and pick up the reins. Only by doing so can we actualize our authority to address the godlessness in our educational system.

ADULTERY, SODOMY, PERVERSION, AND ALL OTHER SEXUAL SINS

All unrepented sexual sins are obvious gateways for demonic entrance, as the law of Moses makes clear. And since Jesus came to fulfill the law (see Matthew 5:17), God's rules have not changed up to the present day. The consequence is absolute: *death* for adultery (see Leviticus 20:10), for incest (see Leviticus 18; 20:12), for homosexual acts or sodomy (see Leviticus 18:22; 20:13; Deuteronomy 23:17; Romans 1:24–28), for bestiality (see Leviticus 18:23), and for all other sexual sins (see Leviticus 18; 20; 1 Corinthians 5:1; 6:9–10, 18–20; 2 Corinthians 12:21; Galatians 5:19; Hebrews 13:4). These sinful acts open people up to demonic influence and control and eventually lead to spiritual death.

The only way to escape the punishment decreed by God is to repent. Confession and repentance (for one's own sin or as an intercessory act of identification on behalf of another) remove the legal right of the enemy to oppress and enslave the one who sins. We must live in the truth. As Paul writes:

Among you there must not be even a hint of sexual immorality, or of any kind of impurity, or of greed, because these are improper for God's holy people. (Ephesians 5:3 NIV)

It is God's will that you should be sanctified: that you should avoid sexual immorality; that each of you should learn to control your own body in a way that is holy and honorable, not in passionate lust like the pagans, who do not know God. (1 Thessalonians 4:3–5 NIV)

FIGHTING, ANGER, HATRED, AND UNFORGIVENESS

We can't quibble with the idea that hatred and outbursts of anger are sinful responses (see, for example, Leviticus 19:17; Ephesians 4:26), although Christians have tried to justify them many times over the centuries. How should we respond instead? Rather than contending, we can bless: "*If someone mistreats you because you are a Christian, don't curse him; pray that God will bless him*" (Romans 12:14 TLB; see also 1 Corinthians 4:12; 1 Peter 3:9).

And you can forgive. Remember the phenomenal power of true forgiveness and let go of your grudges as fast as you can, asking for the Lord's help in doing so. Peter asked Jesus to what extent he should forgive others, and His answer applies to all of us:

> *Then Peter came to Him and said, "Lord, how often shall my brother sin against me, and I forgive him? Up to seven times?" Jesus said to him, "I do not say to you, up to seven times, but up to seventy times seven."* (Matthew 18:21–22)

We are called to live the Sermon on the Mount, turning the opposite cheek (see Matthew 5:39) and walking in a spirit of love, not hate. I remember having a short, clear dream that left a lasting imprint upon my heart. In the dream, various significant figures from church history came and stood before me, and finally a statesman from this generation appeared and stood before me. I heard these words: "You are never too old for the Sermon on the Mount."

We need a love revolution in the church!

REBELLION AGAINST THOSE IN AUTHORITY

This demonic gateway includes disrespect for anyone who is in a position of authority over us, from parents to marriage partners to church leaders to secular rulers to an angel of the Lord. (See, for example, Exodus 20:12; 23:20–21; Leviticus 20:9; 2 Chronicles 36:11–13; 2 Corinthians 6:14–16; Hebrews 13:17.) Remember what Paul wrote to the church in Rome about submission to governmental authority (and this was during the evil Emperor Nero's reign!):

> *Every person is to be in subjection to the governing authorities. For there is no authority except from God, and those which exist are established by God. Therefore whoever resists authority has opposed the ordinance of God; and they who have opposed will receive condemnation upon themselves.... Therefore it is necessary to be in subjection, not only because of wrath, but also for*

conscience' sake. For because of this you also pay taxes, for rulers are servants of God, devoting themselves to this very thing. Render to all what is due them: tax to whom tax is due; custom to whom custom; fear to whom fear; honor to whom honor.

(Romans 13:1–2, 5–7 NASB)

In other words, authority figures do not need to earn the respect of the believers under them in order to be obeyed, as long as they are not asking them to violate God's Word. We need to understand how the kingdom of God works in order to steer clear of sinful responses and their spiritual implications.

With Jesus as our primary example, we must be willing to suffer persecution as we show respect for even threatening authority figures. It is the only way to avoid opening a gateway to the forces of evil.

Submit yourselves for the Lord's sake to every human institution, whether to a king as the one in authority, or to governors as sent by him for the punishment of evildoers and the praise of those who do right. For such is the will of God that by doing right you may silence the ignorance of foolish men. Act as free men, and do not use your freedom as a covering for evil, but use it as bondslaves of God. Honor all people, love the brotherhood, fear God, honor the king. Servants, be submissive to your masters with all respect, not only to those who are good and gentle, but also to those who are unreasonable. For this finds favor, if for the sake of conscience toward God a person bears up under sorrows when suffering unjustly. For what credit is there if, when you sin and are harshly treated, you endure it with patience? But if when you do what is right and suffer for it you patiently endure it, this finds favor with God.

(1 Peter 2:13–20 NASB)

Even if an authority figure behaves in a way that might provoke us to a sinful response (such as anger, hatred, rebellion, evil talk, or retaliation), we must resist the temptation to react as unredeemed people do.

CURSES

As we learn from the Old Testament, curses occur wherever sin and rebellion prevail, but God's blessings come with obedience to His ways. Moses announced to the people of Israel, *"All these blessings shall come upon you and overtake you, because you obey the voice of the LORD your God"* (Deuteronomy 28:2). Then, he listed one specific blessing after another, as God had told him to do. (See verses 3–14.) After this, Moses said, *"But it shall come to pass, if you do not obey the voice of the LORD your God, to observe carefully all His commandments and His statutes which I command you today, that all these curses will come upon you and overtake you"* (Deuteronomy 28:15). Subsequently, he listed the curses that would start to pile up if the people ignored God's voice. (See verses 16–68.)

A curse locks down a sin punishment and allows demonic forces further access to a person or group of people. While keeping their own lives clear of sin, intercessors must be aware of the fact that much of what they pray about comes from entrenched sin, and that includes curses. Curses have a lot to do with relentless relational strife; mental and emotional breakdowns; repeated chronic sickness (especially when there is no clear medical reason); familial patterns of suicides, miscarriages, or unnatural deaths; continual financial insufficiency (especially when income appears to be sufficient); and being accident-prone.

In the face of persistent misfortune, what can we do? Instead of compounding the root sins by an independent spirit or stubborn self-sufficiency, we must ask God's Spirit for insight. Confession of sin and repentance will allow you to break off the power of the evil one. Or, if a curse has resulted from words against you pronounced by a person who essentially represented Satan, God will supply the appropriate prayerful words with which to undo the ungodly covenant with evil.[23]

---

23. For much more about the causes and cures of curses, see my books *Deliverance from Darkness* (see footnote 18) and *The Discerner* (New Kensington, PA: Whitaker House, 2017). Derek Prince wrote the classic book on this subject, *Blessing or Curse: You Can Choose* (Grand Rapids, MI: Chosen Books, 2008). Another tremendous tool is Cindy Jacobs's book *Deliver Us from Evil* (see footnote 21).

CULTIVATE A CLEAN HEART

To confirm and seal our repentance and resistance to sin, we approach the Communion table seeking to come before God with a clean heart. This is not a light matter and must be done with sober judgment, as Paul explains:

> So if anyone eats this bread and drinks from this cup of the Lord in an unworthy manner, he is guilty of sin against the body and the blood of the Lord. That is why a man should examine himself carefully before eating the bread and drinking from the cup. For if he eats the bread and drinks from the cup unworthily, not thinking about the body of Christ and what it means, he is eating and drinking God's judgment upon himself; for he is trifling with the death of Christ. That is why many of you are weak and sick, and some have even died. (1 Corinthians 11:27–30 TLB)

Taking Communion with our brothers and sisters in Christ is another way of closing the gateway to demonic influence. Again, Paul clarifies why: "*You cannot drink the cup of the Lord and the cup of demons; you cannot partake of the Lord's table and of the table of demons*" (1 Corinthians 10:21).

Once, when I was leading a prophetic intercessory gathering, the Holy Spirit spoke very clearly to me concerning our weapons of spiritual warfare. In my spirit, I heard the following: "Communion, the Lord's Supper, is one of the highest and most overlooked weapons of spiritual warfare." After that, I purchased a small traveling Communion set and took it with me on every major ministry trip, partaking of Communion every day and declaring what the blood of Jesus has done. I would encourage you to pray and find the Lord's application of this idea in your own life.

As believers—especially as believers who are intercessors—we must value wisdom and "*walk circumspectly,*" as the King James version puts it: "*See then that you walk circumspectly, not as fools but as wise, redeeming the time, because the days are evil. Therefore do not be unwise, but understand what the will of the Lord is*" (Ephesians 5:15–17).

DEFEATING DEMONIC STRONGHOLDS

To sum up, as intercessors, we need to know how God's king-dom works. And a crucial part of that knowledge comes from under-standing how our personal sins and the sins of others give entrance to demonic oppression. Humble confessions of sin make for powerful prayers because they help to bring down the iniquitous foundations upon which the enemy builds his control. The late C. Peter Wagner summarized this idea well:

> [When] demonic strongholds...exist in a nation or a city,... what can be done about it?
>
> Just as in the case of demonized individuals, if sin is present, repentance is called for; if curses are in effect, they need to be broken....
>
> ...Nehemiah and Daniel give us examples of godly persons who felt the burden for the sins of their nations.
>
> Hearing that Jerusalem's wall was broken down..., Nehemiah wept, fasted, and prayed. He confessed the sins of the children of Israel in general, seeking to remit the sins of the entire nation. He said, *"Both my father's house and I have sinned"* (Neh. 1:6). Here is an example of one person, under an anointing of God, meaningfully confessing the sins of an entire nation.... His prayers obviously had some effect, and God opened doors that only His power could open for the walls and the city to be rebuilt.
>
> Daniel...confessed the sins of his people in detail.... Later he said he had confessed *"my sin and the sin of my people"* (Dan. 9:20).
>
> It is important to note that both Nehemiah and Daniel, while they were standing before God on behalf of their entire nation, confessed not only the corporate sins of their people, but also their individual sins. Those who remit the sins of nations must not fail to identify personally with the sins that

were or are being committed even though they might not per-sonally be as guilty of them as some other sins.[24]

We must walk faithfully and humbly, day by day, always looking to Jesus, *"the pioneer and perfecter"* (Hebrews 12:2 NIV) of our faith. It is a narrow road, and it can be difficult to stay on it, but I have walked too far with Him to turn back now. How about you?

TARGET PRACTICE

I come to You, gracious Father, in Jesus's mighty name, and I declare that all power and authority in heaven and on earth has been given to Jesus, and that He has delegated authority to His disciples. I call forth the Spirit of revelation to increase in my life, so that I can discern the plans of the enemy. Not only do I want to expose demonic gateways, but I also want to close them completely. Continue to lead me into the truth that sets captives free so that Your kingdom can come on earth as it is in heaven. Amen and amen! (See Matthew 28:18–20; John 8:31–32.)

---

24. C. Peter Wagner, *Warfare Prayer* (Shippensburg, PA: Destiny Image, 1992, 2001, rev. 2009), 124–125.

7

CONFESSING
GENERATIONAL SIN

*"O God of hosts, turn again now, we beseech You; look down
from heaven and see, and take care of this vine, even the shoot
which Your right hand has planted, and on the son whom You
have strengthened for Yourself. It is burned with fire, it is cut
down; they perish at the rebuke of Your countenance.
Let Your hand be upon the man of Your right hand, upon the son
of man whom You made strong for Yourself. Then we shall not
turn back from You; revive us, and we will call upon Your name.
O LORD God of hosts, restore us; cause Your face
to shine upon us, and we will be saved."*
—Psalm 80:14–19 (NASB)

In chapter 5, I touched on the amazing power of confession when I
mentioned Daniel's confession of the sins of his exiled people. In writings on prayer in the past twenty years or so, this type of confession has
been referred to as "identificational repentance" or "identification in
intercession." I have only recently formulated a phrase that I have been
using, referring to it as "ambassadorial intercession."

We are ambassadors of a spiritual sphere of delegated authority,
or rule. In prayer, we represent not only ourselves, but also our families, our cities, our places of employment, our ethnic heritage, and

perhaps, at times, even our nations. This is commonly expressed as "confessing generational sin." (It is called "generational" sin because of the biblical reference to the "visitation of the sins of the fathers on their children and children's children." Those sins perpetuate themselves in the actions of the children, and they incur God's punishment. See, for example, Exodus 20:5; Leviticus 26:39; Deuteronomy 5:8–10.)

Although, in some ways, this kind of prayer is called for infrequently, a number of scriptural examples come to mind. In this chapter, we will go into more depth regarding Daniel's confession of generational sin on behalf of the Israelites, and we will also examine the stories of Nehemiah and Ezra.

Although all three of these powerful examples come from the Old Testament, please do not get the impression that the idea of confessing generational sin is limited to the old covenant. Today, under the new covenant, we need to look no further than Jesus's model prayer (the Lord's Prayer) to see it:

> *Our Father which art in heaven, hallowed be thy name. Thy kingdom come, Thy will be done in earth, as it is in heaven. Give us this day our daily bread. And forgive us our debts, as we forgive our debtors. And lead us not into temptation, but deliver us from evil: For thine is the kingdom, and the power, and the glory, for ever. Amen.* (Matthew 6:9–13 KJV)

As I mentioned previously, the Lord's Prayer is a corporate prayer, meant to voice the worship and petitions of a body of believers, as revealed by the use of the plural pronouns *"our Father," "give us," "our daily bread," "forgive us," "lead us not,"* and *"deliver us."* Although we might pray this prayer word for word as we have memorized it, the Lord's Prayer is really meant to be a model prayer, a pattern for how we should pray. That is why Jesus introduced it by saying, *"In this manner, therefore, pray"* (Matthew 6:9).

Once more, it is my strong conviction that Jesus was modeling to His disciples more than an individual devotional prayer. He was demonstrating and teaching a form of intercessory prayer that includes united or corporate prayer and the act of identifying with the needs of society. The personal, devotional dimension of your life and communion with God should already have been taken care of before you enter into the realm of confessing generational sins.

Toward the end of the Lord's Prayer, we say, *"Forgive us our debts, as we forgive our debtors. And lead us not into temptation, but deliver us from evil."* Clearly, by instructing His disciples with this model of prayer, Jesus was showing us how to pray not only for ourselves, but also for other people. Using this prayer as a framework and guide, we can freely pray for anything. And when countless people are praying this way across the face of the earth, together, their prayers will strike many, many targets so that the kingdom of God can advance.

In other words, corporate prayer for corporate needs is powerful, especially when it includes confession of corporate, often generational, sin: "Father, forgive *us*." Such confession was the key to breakthrough for Daniel, Nehemiah, and Ezra.

DANIEL'S EXAMPLE

Exiled to Babylon like most of his countrymen, the Israelite Daniel remained completely faithful to God, despite many attempts by the godless authorities to dissuade him, even in his old age. (Remember the lions' den?) Decades of captivity passed for the Israelites. Hope dimmed that they would ever return home to their own land from their Babylonian captivity.

But one day Daniel was reading from the book of Jeremiah, and the Spirit of the Lord used the words of the prophet to set in motion the deliverance that God had promised His people. It is important to read this passage in its entirety:

> It was now the first year of the reign of King Darius, the son of Ahasuerus. (Darius was a Mede but became king of the Chaldeans.) In that first year of his reign, I, Daniel, learned from the book of Jeremiah the prophet that Jerusalem must lie desolate for seventy years. So I earnestly pleaded with the Lord God to

end our captivity and send us back to our own land. As I prayed,
I fasted and wore rough sackcloth, and I sprinkled myself with
ashes and confessed my sins and those of my people. "O Lord," I
prayed, "you are a great and awesome God; you always fulfill your
promises of mercy to those who love you and keep your laws. But
we have sinned so much; we have rebelled against you and scorned
your commands. We have refused to listen to your servants the
prophets, whom you sent again and again down through the years,
with your messages to our kings and princes and to all the people.
O Lord, you are righteous; but as for us, we are always shame-
faced with sin, just as you see us now; yes, all of us—the men of
Judah, the people of Jerusalem, and all Israel, scattered near and
far wherever you have driven us because of our disloyalty to you.
O Lord, we and our kings and princes and fathers are weighted
down with shame because of all our sins. But the Lord our God
is merciful and pardons even those who have rebelled against him.
O Lord our God, we have disobeyed you; we have flouted all the
laws you gave us through your servants, the prophets. All Israel has
disobeyed; we have turned away from you and haven't listened to
your voice. And so the awesome curse of God has crushed us—the
curse written in the law of Moses your servant. And you have done
exactly as you warned us you would do, for never in all history has
there been a disaster like what happened at Jerusalem to us and
our rulers. Every curse against us written in the law of Moses has
come true; all the evils he predicted—all have come. But even so
we still refuse to satisfy the Lord our God by turning from our sins
and doing right. And so the Lord deliberately crushed us with the
calamity he prepared; he is fair in everything he does, but we would
not obey. O Lord our God, you brought lasting honor to your name
by removing your people from Egypt in a great display of power.
Lord, do it again! Though we have sinned so much and are full of
wickedness, yet because of all your faithful mercies, Lord, please
turn away your furious anger from Jerusalem, your own city, your
holy mountain. For the heathen mock at you because your city lies
in ruins for our sins. O our God, hear your servant's prayer! Listen

as I plead! Let your face shine again with peace and joy upon your desolate sanctuary—for your own glory, Lord. O my God, bend down your ear and listen to my plea. Open your eyes and see our wretchedness, how your city lies in ruins—for everyone knows that it is yours. We don't ask because we merit help, but because you are so merciful despite our grievous sins. O Lord, hear; O Lord, forgive. O Lord, listen to me and act! Don't delay—for your own sake, O my God, because your people and your city bear your name." (Daniel 9:1–19 TLB)

Daniel was pondering the following words of Jeremiah when the Spirit of God enlightened him as to their application (and his own role):

The truth is this: You will be in Babylon for seventy years. But then I will come and do for you all the good things I have promised and bring you home again. For I know the plans I have for you, says the Lord. They are plans for good and not for evil, to give you a future and a hope. In those days when you pray, I will listen. You will find me when you seek me, if you look for me in earnest. Yes, says the Lord, I will be found by you, and I will end your slavery and restore your fortunes; I will gather you out of the nations where I sent you and bring you back home again to your own land.
(Jeremiah 29:10–14 TLB)

Even though his heart leapt at the realization that these words applied to the very conditions in which he found himself, Daniel did not respond presumptuously. Rather, he sought God's Spirit for the next step. What did it mean to pray and to seek Him in earnest? Were blockades in the way? What more could he possibly do than he had already done?

First, he laid aside self-justification and pride—what I think of as the "publican (tax collector) versus Pharisee syndrome." (See Luke 18:9–13.) Daniel himself had been as righteous as possible in every regard. Personally, he had not committed any sin that should have incurred the lifelong captivity that he had suffered along with the other exiles. Nevertheless, he set his face to pray with humility as if he himself had sinned, confessing the people's sin as his own. (See Daniel 9:3–17.) They were his people, after all; he was part of them. He did not claim any exemption from sin-guilt because of his special status. He was acting, therefore, as an ambassador in prayer on their corporate behalf.

Then, he took it a step further and pleaded with the Lord for mercy and deliverance—based not only on his heartfelt confession, but also on the great name of the Lord. (See Daniel 9:18–19.) Fasting, sackcloth, ashes—all spoke of humility before an awesome, sovereign God. Once more we see that, setting aside his own excellent moral character and constancy, Daniel simply confessed the sin of the Israelites as his own. He may well have known these words of Isaiah: *"All we like sheep have gone astray; we have turned every one to his own way"* (Isaiah 53:6 KJV).

And, as the apostle James wrote centuries later, *"Mercy triumphs over judgment"* (James 2:13). God, the great Judge, is a God of unfailing compassion, and Daniel knew it. Therefore, he could end his prayer with these climactic words: *"O Lord, hear; O Lord, forgive. O Lord, listen to me and act! Don't delay—for your own sake, O my God, because your people and your city bear your name"* (Daniel 9:19 TLB). By entering into the guilt of his people, standing in the gap, and confessing their sin as his own, Daniel's prayers struck the bull's-eye. Invisible spiritual forces were set in motion. Before the prophesied seventy years were up, the impossible became possible and captives were returning safely to their own land. This is strategic spiritual warfare, which removes demonic hindrances through the power of confessing generational sins. Daniel left us a great example that we can follow today.

NEHEMIAH'S EXAMPLE

Under the anointing of God, another man, Nehemiah, meaningfully confessed the sins of an entire nation. He was a Hebrew who, during the Babylonian captivity, was cupbearer to the Persian King Artaxerxes. Some think he was a priest as well. In any case, he held an esteemed position in the court. Still, his body was in exile while his heart yearned for Jerusalem, which was in ruins. One day, he received an eyewitness report about the deplorable state of affairs in Jerusalem, and it upset him greatly. He could not rest until the city was restored:

> So it was, when I heard these words, that I sat down and wept, and mourned for many days; I was fasting and praying before the God of heaven. And I said: "I pray, LORD God of heaven, O great and awesome God, You who keep Your covenant and mercy with those who love You and observe Your commandments, please let Your ear be attentive and Your eyes open, that You may hear the prayer of Your servant which I pray before You now, day and night, for the children of Israel Your servants, and confess the sins of the children of Israel which we have sinned against You. Both my father's house and I have sinned. We have acted very corruptly against You, and have not kept the commandments, the statutes, nor the ordinances which You commanded Your servant Moses. Remember, I pray, the word that You commanded Your servant Moses, saying, 'If you are unfaithful, I will scatter you among the nations; but if you return to Me, and keep My commandments and do them, though some of you were cast out to the farthest part of the heavens, yet I will gather them from there, and bring them to the place which I have chosen as a dwelling for My name.' Now these are Your servants and Your people, whom You have redeemed by Your great power, and by Your strong hand. O Lord, I pray, please let Your ear be attentive to the prayer of Your servant, and to the prayer of Your servants who desire to fear Your name; and let Your servant prosper this day, I pray, and grant him mercy in the sight of this man [the king]."   (Nehemiah 1:4–11)

Nehemiah's prayer is a perfect example of both confessing others' sins and reminding God of His promises—which is such an important function of an intercessor. (See chapter 4 of this book, "Reminding God of His Word.") He reminded God of His prophetic promise to Moses and then made an appeal to the Lord on the basis of His redemptive work. He also implored God for favor with the king and asked for success in his endeavor.

Subsequent to his prayer, Nehemiah was permitted to return to Jerusalem from exile to rebuild the wall of the city. Then, after he successfully oversaw the rebuilding of the wall in a phenomenal fifty-two days, he was appointed the governor of Judah. (See Nehemiah 2:1–8; 5:14; 6:15.) Amazing prophetic promises of destiny had been revealed, hindrances had been uncovered, and then Nehemiah, among others, stood in the gap identifying and confessing the Israelites' sins so that they could see God's purposes for His people in their generation being fulfilled.

EZRA'S EXAMPLE

Before the time Nehemiah went back to Jerusalem, Ezra had been allowed to return, taking with him 1,754 of the once-exiled Jews. He brought with him a number of priests and Levites, and his purpose was to restore the worship of God. (See Ezra 7:1–10; 8:1–20.) At first, his efforts seemed successful, but then the newly returned settlers began to adopt the heathen ways of the people around them; even the priests and Levites were intermarrying with them. This violated multiple ordinances according to their faith.

When Ezra heard about this, he was appalled and grieved in the extreme. (See Ezra 9:1–5.) Those who also *"trembled at the words of the God of Israel"* (verse 4) surrounded him, fasting and mourning. Then Ezra began to cry out to God as a priestly spokesman, shouldering the burden of the iniquity of the others and weeping bitter, repentant prayers:

> *O my God, I am ashamed; I blush to lift up my face to you, for our sins are piled higher than our heads and our guilt is as boundless as the heavens. Our whole history has been one of sin; that is why we and our kings and our priests were slain by the heathen kings—we were captured, robbed, and disgraced, just as we are today. But now we have been given a moment of peace, for you have permitted a few of us to return to Jerusalem from our exile. You have given us*

a moment of joy and new life in our slavery. For we were slaves, but in your love and mercy you did not abandon us to slavery; instead, you caused the kings of Persia to be favorable to us. They have even given us their assistance in rebuilding the Temple of our God and in giving us Jerusalem as a walled city in Judah. And now, O God, what can we say after all of this? For once again we have abandoned you and broken your laws! The prophets warned us that the land we would possess was totally defiled by the horrible practices of the people living there. From one end to the other it is filled with corruption. You told us not to let our daughters marry their sons, and not to let our sons marry their daughters, and not to help those nations in any way. You warned us that only if we followed this rule could we become a prosperous nation and forever leave that prosperity to our children as an inheritance. And now, even after our punishment in exile because of our wickedness (and we have been punished far less than we deserved), and even though you have let some of us return, we have broken your commandments again and intermarried with people who do these awful things. Surely your anger will destroy us now until not even this little remnant escapes. O Lord God of Israel, you are a just God; what hope can we have if you give us justice as we stand here before you in our wickedness? (Ezra 9:6–15 TLB)

Once again, we see an example of someone whose own character and behavior were above reproach, but who humbled himself before God, repenting for the sins of his wayward people. Just like Daniel and Nehemiah, he did so with an absence of self-justification, moving smoothly into an ambassadorial role as he represented his people before God.

And once more, those prayers made a significant difference. The men agreed to divorce their heathen wives and send them back to their families. Now, that had to have created a lot of turmoil, emotional upheaval, and genuine hardship. But nothing gets left out when God's spotlight gets turned on! It took three full months to complete the process, and Ezra continued to mourn and pray. But in the end, their repentance and reform were complete.

MODERN-DAY EXAMPLES

From time to time, quiet spiritual breakthroughs are initiated by means of generational confession of sin and repentance. When we recognize enemy strongholds in a region or group of people, we should be alert to identify old wounds and unresolved guilt. After identifying with the aggrieved people and acknowledging the sins and injustices that were committed against them, we can repent for long-ago sins and even ask for forgiveness.

In the United States, this is what has taken place in several localities with regard to the past abuse of native American tribes. *Abuse* is a general term that covers everything from uncharitable, prejudicial treatment to atrocities such as the slaughter of innocent women and children. When prayers and statements of reconciliation include modern representatives of both sides, long-overdue confession and repentance open a channel through which forgiveness can flow. True reconciliation replaces bitter animosity. Healing comes to the descendants of both the native Americans and their persecutors—and to the territory as a whole.

In my city of Nashville, Tennessee, another issue took center stage: prostitution. In the past, especially during the American Civil War, the city acquired a bawdy reputation, even legalizing prostitution for a time. As the growing city began to acquire a new reputation, that of "Music City, U.S.A.," some intercessors began to wonder why so much of the music, which had started out as gospel music, had become corrupted and tainted. Much of the country and western music portrayed unredeemed human nature, and the contemporary Christian music and old gospel music could not counterbalance it. Eventually, it was determined that the sin history of the city had something to do with it. This led to prayers of repentance by various groups for the way the gospel had been "prostituted" through the music industry.

Having been one who has personally stood in the gap for Nashville for over twenty years, I believe that I am now seeing a cleansing in this influential, artistic city. We may even be on the threshold of an entirely new "Jesus People" movement that will begin right in the heart of this place. From my vantage point, it appears that God has used one generation to identify the problems and hindrances and a subsequent generation to release the prophetic solution through prayer. This joining of the generations is what revival pastor Lou Engle and I wrote about in our book *The Call of the Elijah Revolution*.[25]

Let's look at another example from recent times. Near Pasadena, California, in the early 1990s, a group of intercessors asked forgiveness on behalf of their city forefathers, who had named a dam Devil's Gate. Here is the story as told by Lou Engle, who resided in Pasadena at the time:

> The original water source of Pasadena and Los Angeles is a dam bearing the name of Devil's Gate.... A 1947 *Pasadena Star-News* article said, "It's true [that] Devil's Gate is named because of the resemblance of the rocks to his Satanic Majesty."... The Lord gave me a word from the passage where Elisha poured salt into the water source of Jericho and healed the contaminated waters (II Kings 2:19–22). Then it struck me with much force to go pour salt as an act of prophetic intercession into the stream at Devil's Gate, to ask forgiveness on behalf of our forefathers for naming it such, to break the curse and ask for revival to be poured out on Pasadena.
>
> We took our intercession team to the place and did precisely that. We asked God to release rivers of life and fruitfulness into the parched lives of thousands. At that time the drought in Southern California had been going on for five years.... Eight days later, the rains began to pour so much that the newspapers called the month "Miracle March."[26]

25. James W. Goll and Lou Engel, *The Call of the Elijah Revolution* (Shippensburg, PA: Destiny Image, 2008).

26. Steve Hawthorne and Graham Kendrick, *Prayerwalking: Praying On-Site with Insight* (Lake Mary, FL: Charisma House, 1993), 115–116.

Subsequently, the city of Pasadena began to restore to the area the original native name of Hahamongna, which means "Flowing Waters, Fruitful Valley." The city did experience a spiritual revival in the early 1990s, after sustained meetings resulted in the formation of a local church called Harvest Rock Church (now HRock Church) under the leadership of pastors Ché Ahn, Lou Engle, and others. Their efforts eventually resulted in the emergence of an apostolic network called Harvest International Ministries, in which I have the honor of participating to this day.

IDENTIFYING WITH THE SINS

Just as Jerusalem had another chance to survive and thrive thanks to Ezra and Nehemiah, so do our cities and their institutions—once concerned intercessors obey God's summons to step into the gap with generational confession and repentance.

John Dawson, who has served in many leadership roles with Youth With A Mission (YWAM), clarifies what this means in his book *Taking Our Cities for God*:

Through repentance, reconciliation, and prayer, the present generation can work to repair the broken-down walls of the city....

In responding to the broken heart of God, we must identify with the sins of the city in personal and corporate repentance. When Nehemiah prayed for the restoration of Jerusalem, he did not pray for the city as if he were not part of it. He said, "I and this people have sinned." (See Nehemiah 1:6–7.)...

...You may be a righteous person who is not involved in any direct way with the vices present in your city.... [But] we can all identify with the roots of any given sin....

...The potential for the worst evil lies within each one of us, apart from God's saving grace and the life of Christ within us....

...It is only when God has cleansed my own wicked heart that participation in the redeeming work of intercession becomes possible. It is then that the power to change history is released through prayer....

...As you stand in the gap for your city, allow the Holy Spirit to shine the bright light of truth into the inner rooms of your soul. Run from the religious deceit that would seduce you into believing that you are superior to any person. It is only by the blood of the Lamb and the power of the Spirit that we stand free from the chains of guilt and the sentence of death.[27]

Dawson is credited as the originator of the phrase "identificational repentance," which he popularized in his book *Healing America's Wounds*.[28] As we have seen, identification in intercession is a form of confessing generational sins—anything from the transgressions of your own ancestors to corporate, national sins. By identifying with the sinful parties, you present your prayers as if they are coming from the people's own hearts and mouths. You *identify yourself* with them, coming on your knees before God. Yes, it is painful. It hurts to become an ambassador between sinners and the Judge, compassionately bearing the burden of sin to the throne. Yet as historical wrongs are set right through your repentant prayers, you can move on to pray for mercy and restoration. The blood of Jesus can erase all sin, past or present. What had seemed to be a permanent condition can become temporary.

By combining prophetic revelation, diligent research, and discernment—as led by the Spirit of God—any of us can enter into profound identificational and generational confession and repentance, which are vital to the advancement of God's kingdom. It is a lot more than changing the wording of our prayers from "them" to "us," because we must deeply and humbly identify with the sins of others. We require

---

27. John Dawson, *Taking Our Cities for God* (Lake Mary, FL: Charisma House, 1989, 2001), 55, 143–145, 147–148.
28. John Dawson, *Healing America's Wounds* (Grand Rapids, MI: Baker Publishing Group, 1994).

wisdom from God in order to carry out this kind of intercession. We need God's own loving heart.[29]

I am committed to being an ambassador for Christ, and I invite you to be one, too. Together, let's follow the model prayer of Jesus, confessing generational sin by crying out, "Father, forgive us, for we have sinned!"

TARGET PRACTICE

O heavenly Father, I come to You right now as an ambassador of Christ and of my people. I am grateful to be learning more about the privilege of standing in the gap and confessing generational sin on behalf of others. Thank You for giving us the role models of Daniel, Nehemiah, Ezra, and Jesus Himself. I choose to take my place before the throne of Almighty God in this transforming act of prayer. Thank You, Father! Amen.

---

29. For more on identification in intercession, see my book *Intercession: The Power and Passion to Shape History* (Shippensburg, PA: Destiny Image, 2011).

8

PRAYING ON-SITE
WITH INSIGHT

"Hear my prayer, O Lord; answer my plea because you are faithful to your promises.... I remember the glorious miracles you did in days of long ago. I reach out for you.... Show me where to walk, for my prayer is sincere. Save me from my enemies. O Lord, I run to you to hide me. Help me to do your will, for you are my God. Lead me in good paths, for your Spirit is good."
—Psalm 143:1, 5–6, 8–10 (TLB)

Are you ready for more? I have been taking you on this journey called *Strike the Mark* one step at a time. These chapters reveal a sequence of teachings that build upon one another. Throughout the chapters you have just read, I have been diving more deeply into what I termed in chapter 3 "the faces of prayer." I want you to remember that prayer has many expressions. Although they differ much from one another, all of the prayer anointings are valid and strategic.

What many call "praying on-site with insight" is one of my personal favorites. When I first heard about it, I knew it was for me. By nature, as I mentioned earlier, I am more of a prayer assignment person rather than the more typical prayer room pray-er. Personally, I can find it hard to sit in a room for a protracted period of time. I need to get out and do something!

In fact, from my boyhood, I have combined walking and praying. When I was growing up, I walked along the rural railroad tracks near my home and talked to Jesus. As it turns out, that is called "prayerwalking." Nobody told me about it; I just did it. I kept doing it into my teens and twenties and thirties and forties. I prayerwalked wherever I found myself.

I prayerwalked my university campus when I was a college student. I logged hours of prayerwalking in the streets of Manhattan, New York City. I have prayerwalked in key cities of the former Soviet Union. I have literally walked the walls of Jerusalem late at night. I have prayed on-site at Rees Howell's Bible College of Wales in Swansea, where I received God's commissioning from Howell's son Samuel to a call of "crisis intervention through intercession." Today, I prayerwalk my neighborhood in Franklin, Tennessee, and I have even invited people to join me on Periscope to pray for their neighborhoods (because, remember, we must talk to God about our neighbors before we talk to our neighbors about God)!

I am primarily a prophetic intercessor, and that is how I receive revelatory insights. I only want to pray according to the inspired insights that come from the Holy Spirit. So much the better if I can go out to the very site of what I am praying about. Whether on my own or with other intercessors, I stand on my own two feet in the place I am praying for, even performing prophetic actions such as Lou Engle and his prayer team did at the Devil's Gate dam near Pasadena (described in the previous chapter).

PRAYERWALKING, PRAYING ON-SITE

Across the world, the Spirit of God has been stirring intercessors to pray like this. Some pray while walking their cities, street by street, following prearranged plans. Others prayerwalk only occasionally, under a special anointing. They pray everything from general "blessing" prayers to finely tuned, detailed prayers that displace demonic spirits of darkness. They do not all necessarily pray expecting to see immediate or even swift results, because many have faith for the long haul that reaches into the future. As Steve Hawthorne and Graham Kendrick put it in their book *Prayerwalking*, "Most of these pray-ers don't imagine themselves to be just bravely holding flickering candles toward an overwhelming darkness. Rather, long fuses are being lit for anticipated explosions of God's love."[30]

Intercessors prayerwalk in their own neighborhoods as they move past each house. They spread out to other neighborhoods and commercial districts, campuses and schools. They target specific locations near and far. With the creative help of the Holy Spirit, they come up with a refreshing variety of techniques and strategies for praying on-site with insight.

Their prayers are directed by both inspiration and good, old-fashioned research. In other words, they obtain prayer insights by depending on the guidance of the Spirit as well as by rounding up as much historical and geographical information as possible. Their prayers are very purposeful, not open-ended in terms of subject matter. They are not trying to replace normal prayer meetings or personal times of intercession. The difference is that their prayers are being prayed on the very sites and in the very places where they expect to see them answered.

On-site prayers are perfect for proclaiming God's promises over a region. As they survey the landscape, intercessors can saturate the atmosphere with worship, aligning themselves with God's desires. They may feel led to confess generational sins or geographical transgressions. Because their feet are situated directly on the place they are praying for, they can better identify with its needs. In these cases, intercessors who might otherwise be timid about speaking up in public often feel freer to participate without hesitation.

LIKE ABRAHAM, JOSHUA, AND JESUS

Believe it or not, the idea of praying on-site with insight dates at least as far back as the time of Abraham:

---

30. Hawthorne and Kendrick, *Prayerwalking*, 10.

The LORD said to Abram after Lot had parted from him, "Look around from where you are, to the north and south, to the east and west. All the land that you see I will give to you and your offspring forever. I will make your offspring like the dust of the earth, so that if anyone could count the dust, then your offspring could be counted. Go, walk through the length and breadth of the land, for I am giving it to you."   (Genesis 13:14–17 NIV)

This is a matter of vision: God told Abraham first to survey the land, and then to walk around on it. By doing so, Abraham not only was able to survey the area, but also, his obedience enabled him to lay claim to it.

Prayerwalking is one of the best ways to lay claim to a place for the kingdom of God. Not long ago, a large group of believers in San Francisco, aided by others from outside the city, prayed and fasted and walked every street in the Bay area. That army of intercessors prayed with fervency and faith—not "flickering-candle-in-the-darkness" prayers, but prayers with a "long fuse." They were praying right on the turf where they expected their prayers to be answered, planting revival seeds with faith, confident that God would hear and respond at some point in the future.

Another precursor to modern-day prayerwalking is recorded in the book of Numbers, when Joshua led a group of Israelites to spy out the land that God had promised to Moses:

When Moses sent them to explore Canaan, he said, "Go up through the Negev and on into the hill country. See what the land is like and whether the people who live there are strong or weak, few or many. What kind of land do they live in? Is it good or bad? What kind of towns do they live in? Are they unwalled or fortified? How is the soil? Is it fertile or poor? Are there trees in it or not? Do your best to bring back some of the fruit of the land."
                (Numbers 13:17–20 NIV)

The group went on foot, surveying the promised territory and its potential fruit as well as the enemy opposition they were likely to face. As it turned out, fear of the opposition won out in most of the men—except for Joshua and Caleb. Those two men had *"a different spirit"* (Numbers 14:24). In due time, forty years later, their positive assessment of the promised land prevailed at last. They followed the Lord fully and faithfully until they saw His promises fulfilled. (See Deuteronomy 1:36; Joshua 14:6–15.)

The Lord Jesus Himself prayed on-site with insight when, for example, He anguished over Jerusalem as He looked out over the city. (See Luke 19:41–44; see also Matthew 23:37; Luke 13:34.) And upon seeing the great needs of the people, He prayed publicly for laborers for the harvest. (See Matthew 9:35–38.) He urged His followers (which includes us) to travel far and wide, praying and preaching everywhere, telling them why: *"He who hears you hears Me, he who rejects you rejects Me, and he who rejects Me rejects Him who sent Me"* (Luke 10:16; see also Luke 10:1–12). If it was good enough for Jesus, then....

WHERE CAN YOU PRAY?

The above examples help to show the purpose and value of praying on-site in an informed way, but by no means do they cover all of the possible kinds of places where you can pray. Just think about it—you can prayerwalk on-site just about anywhere you find yourself. Here, drawn from chapter 9 of Hawthorne and Kendrick's *Prayerwalking*, are ten likely places where you can pray:

WORKPLACES

Have you ever considered prayerwalking through your place of employment? The feasibility of doing this depends upon the kind of place it is and may work best after hours. If you have any Christian coworkers, perhaps they would be interested in praying with you. You could call this "marketplace intercession." Marketplace intercession is on the rise as people catch the vision to influence every sphere of society for the sake of Jesus Christ.

SITES FOR CONSECRATED USE

As you feel led, you can pray for certain properties to be released into (or back into) God's purposes. This is essentially what Joshua did when he vanquished the city of Jericho in one of the greatest prayer-walks of all time. (See Joshua 6.) Do you feel that God wants you to claim the streets of your city for Himself? Perhaps it is time to revive the March for Jesus movement, which united Christians from all backgrounds in Australia, Europe, and North America for a forty-year stretch and which still remains a strong worship and prayer force in South America.

In a personal application, my wife, Michal Ann, and I felt in our hearts that the Lord had some acreage south of Nashville that was meant to become a home for our family. Though we had little money, we dared to dream big and to believe that this particular charming farm in the country was indeed set aside for us as a place where the six of us could spread our wings. At one point, even though the property was not on the market, we drove our entire family in our van out to this location. We prayerwalked the twenty-nine acres and declared that it was ours. In other words, we consecrated the land to the Lord through prayer. The outcome? The property suddenly came on the market, a surprise financial gift came in the mail, and we bought it. We lived there for thirteen years, raising our family to dream big!

OVERLOOKS AND HIGH PLACES

Elevated sites from which prayers can be offered on behalf of the city or region in view are not only ideal positions for strong prayers and proclamations, but are also often like spiritual "high places" where ungodly acts have occurred. The overlook itself can be reclaimed for the kingdom of God even as the vista around it can. A high place is the best place to offer up intense and joyful praise and worship as the site is repossessed for God.

I remember heading up the intercessory prayer teams for an outdoor crusade in Haiti held by power evangelist Mahesh Chavda. Late one night, the Lord directed me to take a select group of men to a high point overlooking the capital city and to pray on-site with insight. The burden of the Lord came upon us for the removal of an ungodly political regime. Travail gripped us as though we were in labor for the promise to come into being. The result? Soon, the evil ruler was dislodged and a window of opportunity was granted for change to come to the most impoverished nation in the Western hemisphere. Our prayers had struck the mark!

SITES OF TRAGIC EVENTS

As soon as you hear of a crime or a disaster, you can gather intercessors to go as close to the epicenter as possible to counter the tragedy with blessings. Intercessors have done this in a concerted way at public sites where murders have taken place, and the murder rate in their city has plummeted dramatically. Such sites may be good places for identification repentance and pleas for mercy. Spilled blood ever speaks before the Lord for vengeance (see Genesis 4:9–12), but we can plead the blood of Jesus and declare, *"Mercy triumphs over judgment"* (James 2:13; see also Hebrews 12:24).

Over the years, several different ministries have conducted prayerwalks and rallies along the historic Trail of Tears, where thousands of Native Americans died as they were marched from their homelands by the U.S. government. These prayerwalks and rallies resulted in official apologies from sitting governmental representatives and acts of restitution. My late wife and I participated in many of these prayer initiatives, as well as in the day of prayer for the Cherokee tribe that was held in Oklahoma.

PLACES WITH EVIL NAMES

The world over, places have been named for disasters, criminals, and even Satan himself (as in the case of Devil's Gate mentioned in chapter 7 of this book). If you discern that the time is right, ask the Lord if He wants you to lay claim to godly alternatives and to weaken the bonds that link the old name to darkness.

Among many others, I prayed that the city of Leningrad would be loosed from the grip of communism and that its original (prophetic) name of Saint Petersburg would be returned to it. Over time, as communism became past-tense ("commun-wasm"), a door to change and freedom opened over the biblical "land of the north." Today, Saint Petersburg carries its original name.

SITES OF PAST SIN

In the previous chapter, I mentioned how Nashville had been tainted by the past sin of legalized prostitution and how local intercessors learned how to pray about it. As Hawthorne and Kendrick explained, "In the same way that sins of parents can have ongoing consequences for [the next generations], the cumulative sin of one generation can reverberate throughout society for generations. The rampant sin of today may be yesterday's sin multiplied."[31] Sins that were committed at certain sites or neighborhoods might have given entrance to demonic powers, and one of the best ways to counter the evil is to visit the site, cleanse it by pleading the blood of Jesus, and replace curses with blessings. Some of the intercessors of the greater Nashville region gathered at the Cumberland River to call forth a cleansing of the waters that flow from the city into the world. We declared that Music City, U.S.A., would become "Worship City" to the world.

SITES OF ONGOING SIN

What can you do about your city's "underbelly" of sin? With God guiding you, you can pray on-site with insight. You can go to the red-light district or visit the parks where illegal drugs are sold. You can target gambling operations. In particular, you can pray prayers of confession and repentance. As with sites of past sin, make it a point to confess and repent on behalf of the residents and visitors. Pray for God's light to shine there. Some intercessors share the Lord's Supper, or Communion, as a way of blessing such a site. Often, these consecrated believers will declare the benefits of the shed blood of Jesus.

It could be said, of course, that every place inhabited by fallen humankind is a site of ongoing sin. My friend Norm Stone thought so. In the 1980s and again at the turn of the century, Norm and a few

31. Hawthorne and Kendrick, *Prayerwalking*, 116.

friends trekked across the continental United States seven times as a prophetic, intercessory act, calling forth compassion and repentance for the national sin of abortion. Rallies were held at various locations where prayers, proclamations, and promises about a culture of life were declared.

EVIL STRONGHOLDS

An evil stronghold may be an identifiable geographical region, but more importantly, it will be characterized by people who have been deceived and blinded by demonic powers. When you feel led to target a place from which evil seems to be flowing, bring with you not only your godly authority but also a heart for the people who are being held as prisoners there. Pray that the Spirit would *"open their eyes so that they may turn from darkness to light and from the dominion of Satan to God, that they may receive forgiveness of sins and an inheritance among those who have been sanctified by faith in* [Christ]" (Acts 26:18 NASB).

CITY "GATES"

Very few cities have actual walls and gates anymore, but the effective gates or entrance points of any city can be identified by a combination of prayerful research and direct revelation from God. In ancient times, the city elders governed from seats at the actual entrances to the city, and this practice was modified over time to other seats of leadership, such as city halls, courtrooms, and influential businesses. Ideally, the city gates serve to filter out evil influences while promoting healthy interchange. Intercession to reestablish city gates will include prayers that not only confess the sins of corruption and generational influences, but also declare the prophetic promises for the city's future.

HOW TO ENGAGE

Much more could be said about each of these potential types of places for on-site prayer, as well as possible prayer strategies. When you feel God wants you to tackle the darkness in a particular place, be sure to do your homework first. Your prayers and actions will have real impact only if they are inspired by the Holy Spirit, and you can succeed only if you proceed with careful preparation, most often in the company of others. Do not be surprised if nothing seems to happen. After all, you are lighting what may be a slow fuse for a God-explosion sometime in the future.

Never forget praise and worship—before, during, and after an on-site prayer engagement. Pour out lavish praise. It clears the way, cleanses the atmosphere, and releases God's angels to bind the forces of darkness. Intentional, heartfelt worship positions you under the mighty hand of God—humble and yet confident. Receiving His grace, you can exercise your right to petition Him, asking Him to intervene powerfully in the situation at hand. You can reach into the very heart of God and discover His purposes for a region. Regardless of the darkness of its history, you can declare a bright future as He shows you how to proclaim those purposes.

Combine the insights about how to pray from this chapter with the new insights of the moment as you are led by God's Spirit, and your prayers will be well-aimed and effectual. *"The effectual fervent prayer of a righteous man* [woman, team] *availeth much"* (James 5:16 KJV).

TARGET PRACTICE

Gracious Father, I declare that the shed blood of the Lord Jesus Christ is greater and more powerful than any one-time act of sin or even all ongoing, repeated, sinful activities. Lead me and those I walk with into new levels of revelatory insight. I pray that You will reveal to us Your strategies for how we can pray effectively on behalf of our city. Thank You for teaching us how to pray on-site with insight. In Jesus's wonderful name, amen and amen!

9

NO COMMON
GROUND ALLOWED

"The ruler of this world is coming, and he has nothing in Me."
—John 14:30

As a prayer warrior, would you consider yourself a good "wrestler"? Or do you run at the first sign of contention, having lost battles too often? I hope that you, along with all other believers and intercessors, can recognize yourself in these words of Paul: *"We do not wrestle against flesh and blood, but against principalities, against powers, against the rulers of the darkness of this age, against spiritual hosts of wickedness in the heavenly places"* (Ephesians 6:12).

When Paul says *"we,"* this is all-inclusive language. He means every believer in Christ, regardless of gender, age, physique, or fighting ability—we are all called to be wrestlers in God's kingdom. We do not get to decide whether or not we will fight. We belong to the Lord Jesus, and that fact automatically sets us in opposition to His foes. We were born in the midst of battle and we were born for battle!

PRINCIPALITIES AND POWERS

What are we fighting? We are contending against the powers of darkness wherever we find them. We fight them even though it is difficult to see them. For the most part, they are invisible. Whether or not we have been graced with the gift of discerning of spirits (see 1 Corinthians 12:10), we are fighting principalities, powers, rulers of darkness, and spiritual hosts of wickedness.

We do not wrestle against flesh-and-blood people. But be certain that we do wrestle. Some theologians seem to wrongly interpret Scriptures such as Ephesians 6:12 in a passive manner: "we wrestle not"—period! Well, it is true that we do not wrestle with people, but we *do* wrestle with the powers of darkness. To keep us from lashing out at the wrong targets, we need God's wisdom and insight, His direction and correction. He is the only one who can keep us from wrong-headed applications of battle strategies or from waging warfare in a presumptuous way. He is the only one who can protect us and keep us from being another spiritual warfare casualty.

The Lord urges us back into the battle when we might prefer to avoid it, hoping He will do all our fighting for us. Instead, He coaches and equips us for actual hand-to-hand combat, which is what we are called to. Never mind that the enemy is using flaming missiles and fiery arrows (see Ephesians 6:16), which he shoots at us from a distance. He is afraid, so he tries to make us afraid, too—and to keep us from unveiling his schemes. He knows that if we get close enough, we will discern his tactics, and, even though he will fight back, we will be armed and able to gain the upper hand. He knows that, with God's expert assistance, we can win.[32]

GOD: A MAN OF WAR

In many places in Scripture, God is presented as a warrior, a commander of an army. Here are some examples:

> The LORD is a man of war; the LORD is His name.
>
> (Exodus 15:3)

---

32. For more detail about these subjects, please refer to my books *Deliverance from Darkness* (see footnote 18) and *The Discerner* (see footnote 23).

And it came to pass, when Joshua was by Jericho, that he lifted his eyes and looked, and behold, a Man stood opposite him with His sword drawn in His hand. And Joshua went to Him and said to Him, "Are You for us or for our adversaries?" So He said, "No, but as Commander of the army of the LORD I have now come." And Joshua fell on his face to the earth and worshiped, and said to Him, "What does my Lord say to His servant?" (Joshua 5:13–14)

I have commanded My consecrated ones, I have even called My mighty warriors, My proudly exulting ones, to execute My anger. A sound of tumult on the mountains, like that of many people! A sound of the uproar of kingdoms, of nations gathered together! The LORD of hosts is mustering the army for battle. (Isaiah 13:3–4 NASB)

From the very beginning, humankind has been enmeshed in the enmity between God and Satan:

And I will put enmity between thee and the woman, and between thy seed and her seed; it shall bruise thy head, and thou shalt bruise his heel. (Genesis 3:15 KJV)

The God of peace will soon crush Satan under your feet. The grace of our Lord Jesus be with you. (Romans 16:20 NIV)

Jesus explained that because of the commitment and cost of following Him, He brings strife, and we must accept this as fact:

Do not think that I came to bring peace on earth. I did not come to bring peace but a sword. For I have come to "set a man against his father, a daughter against her mother, and a daughter-in-law against her mother-in-law"; and "a man's enemies will be those of his own household." He who loves father or mother more than Me is not worthy of Me. And he who loves son or daughter more than Me is not worthy of Me. And he who does not take his cross and follow after Me is not worthy of Me. (Matthew 10:34–38)

Yes, you and I were born for spiritual battle. It is an inescapable fact. If we shrink from this call and only try to find peace in the world around us, we may find ourselves on the wrong side of the battle:

You are like an unfaithful wife who loves her husband's enemies. Don't you realize that making friends with God's enemies—the evil pleasures of this world—makes you an enemy of God? I say it again, that if your aim is to enjoy the evil pleasure of the unsaved world, you cannot also be a friend of God. (James 4:4 TLB)

It will not end well for the forces of darkness. We need to keep standing with God, armed for battle:

God took away Satan's power to accuse you of sin, and God openly displayed to the whole world Christ's triumph at the cross where your sins were all taken away. (Colossians 2:15 TLB)

Since the children have flesh and blood, he too shared in their humanity so that by his death he might break the power of him who holds the power of death—that is, the devil.
(Hebrews 2:14 NIV)

Therefore, take up the full armor of God, so that you will be able to resist in the evil day, and having done everything, to stand firm.
(Ephesians 6:13 NASB)

We know that at the end, even if we are battle-weary, the Lord of hosts will be the absolute Victor:

For it is written: "As I live, says the LORD, every knee shall bow to Me, and every tongue shall confess to God."
(Romans 14:11; see Isaiah 45:23)

"Every knee" means *every* knee: Every enemy of God will have to bend the knee to Him and acknowledge His lordship. Every one of His rivals will have to capitulate. Every "-ism" ever known to civilization will have to surrender to the Name—communism, capitalism, humanism, atheism, conservatism, liberalism, materialism, universalism....

PULLING DOWN STRONGHOLDS

Our role in the fight has been specified for us, with divine assistance guaranteed when we step into our battle position:

> For though we walk in the flesh, we do not war according to the flesh. For the weapons of our warfare are not carnal but mighty in God for pulling down strongholds, casting down arguments and every high thing that exalts itself against the knowledge of God, bringing every thought into captivity to the obedience of Christ.
>
> (2 Corinthians 10:3–5)

The *"weapons of our warfare"* do not depend on our own strength, because they are *"mighty in God for pulling down strongholds."* In His strength, we demolish any defensive structure that defies God. As I noted earlier, we are not contending against individuals, but against power structures. Here Paul calls them *"strongholds,"* or "fortresses."

How should we picture strongholds? The Greek word translated as *"strongholds"* in the above passage is *ochuróma*. It refers to a strong-walled, fortified, military fortress and "is used figuratively of a false argument in which a person seeks 'shelter' ('a safe place') to escape reality."[33] The word can be used to refer to personal strongholds or, more widely, to trends and assumptions of thought.

Ed Silvoso, head of Harvest Evangelism, has successfully led intercessors in his native Argentina and many other nations to come against invisible strongholds that get in the way of evangelism. He knows that we cannot tackle strongholds outside ourselves until we have dealt with the ones in our own minds. He defines such inner strongholds as follows: "A spiritual stronghold is a mind-set impregnated with hopelessness that causes us to accept as unchangeable, situations that we know are contrary to the will of God."[34]

Youth With a Mission (YWAM) Bible teacher Dean Sherman adds this:

---

33. See *Strong's Exhaustive Concordance*, #G3794, *ochuróma* and Pamela McLaughlin, *Chosen Treasures* (self-published, 2013), 116.
34. Ed Silvoso, *That None Should Perish* (Ventura, CA: Regal Books, 1994), 154.

I have heard people use the term *strongholds* to refer to humanism, Islam, communism, and other religions and institutions. However, in II Corinthians, *strongholds* does not refer to massive, complex systems, human or demonic. Here it refers to the strongholds of the mind. These strongholds are castles in the air built up in our minds through wrong thinking—through unbelieving, depressed, fearful, and negative thinking.

Two mental strongholds are extremely common today among Christians and non-Christians alike: thoughts of inferiority, and thoughts of condemnation.

Inferior thoughts constantly tell us, "You're not big enough. You're not smart enough. You don't look good. You're not really making it in life. You're worthless." These barbs keep us competing with and envying others.

Satan also accuses, "You're not pleasing God. You are not spiritual enough. You do not read your Bible enough. You're not close to God." These thoughts make us feel as if we can never break through into the fresh air and sunshine of God's approval. Some Christians live every day of their lives in dreary condemnation.

These two strongholds must be cast down through spiritual warfare, as we refuse them and instead accept what God says about us in the Bible.[35]

As you conquer these mental strongholds, you will grow in your faith, the gifts of the Holy Spirit, and the anointing to combat other ungodly beliefs patterns. A warrior never quits, and a warrior continues to take new territory in Christ Jesus.

PROGRESSIVE SPHERES OF AUTHORITY

Yes, faithfulness brings increase. As you are faithful in one sphere, you will graduate to the next. Always keep in mind that you qualify for

35. Dean Sherman, *Spiritual Warfare for Every Christian* (Seattle, WA: YWAM Publishing, 1990), 52.

an increase in spiritual authority when you are first faithful in smaller responsibilities, in the natural realms of life, and with what belongs to others. (See Luke 16:10–12.) These are the words and principles of Jesus!

Thus, as we grow in personal responsibility, we will also grow in our capacity and stewardship for a larger sphere of responsibility. You could term this "growing from personal to progressive spheres of authority." Let us demonstrate faithfulness in the following spheres of influence:

1. Our individual lives
2. Our family relationships
3. Our relationship to the church
4. Our responsibility to our cities
5. Our concern and care for our nation

PROGRESSIVE POSSESSION OF PURITY

We must also realize that the greater the spiritual battle, the greater the need for a pure heart and mind. Holiness is essential if we are to be effective in long-term spiritual warfare.

Psalm 24 asks us this pertinent question: "Who may ascend into the hill of the LORD?" (verse 3). The answer comes quickly: "He who has clean hands and a pure heart" (verse 5). It takes an internal heart of purity to produce external works of our hands that are acceptable to the Lord. Unseen purity results in visible fruit! What a truth! What a reality!

Pastor and author Terry Crist writes, "If you are going to gather people for battle, you must free them from their captivity.... You can't possess the land *without* until you possess the land *within*."[36]

Thus, the first battlefield we must win is the battlefield of our own minds, and as we make progress and gain victories, we become better

---

36. Terry Crist, *Interceding Against the Powers of Darkness* (Tulsa, OK: Terry Crist Ministries, 1990), 19.

prepared to face territorial strongholds that control the thoughts and actions of groups of people. George Otis Jr. broadly defines the force of these strongholds as "repelling light" and "exporting darkness."[37] Such strongholds can be categorized as personal, mental, ideological, occultic, social, demonic, sectarian, iniquitous, and other types.[38]

Could it be that part of the reason Jesus was so effective in spiritual warfare in His wilderness confrontation with Satan was that He recognized the "law of purification"? Jesus could stand in complete power and authority to deal effectively with the strongholds of the oppressor because there was no common ground between Him and His adversary! His heart was pure. Jesus said to His disciples, "*The ruler of this world is coming, and he has nothing in Me*" (John 14:30).

Again, as author Terry Crist states:

> When the devil struck at Jesus, there was nothing whatsoever in Him to receive the "hit." When Satan examined Him, there was nothing for him to find. Jesus and Satan had no relationship one to another, no common ground. There was nothing in Jesus' life that had agreement with the works of darkness! One reason so many ministers and intercessors have been spiritually "hit" by the fiery darts of the enemy is because they have not responded to the law of purification."[39]

A WORD OF WISDOM

As you function as an intercessor and engage in spiritual warfare, keep in mind that not every battle is for you. Yes, some are for you. Some are for others. Some are for today. Some are for another day (or even year). For some battles, you are called to the frontlines. For

37. George Otis Jr., "An Overview of Spiritual Mapping," in *Breaking Spiritual Strongholds in Your City*, ed. C. Peter Wagner, 42 (Shippensburg, PA: Destiny Image, 2015).

38. Cindy Jacobs, "Dealing with Strongholds," in *Breaking Spiritual Strongholds in Your City*, ed. C. Peter Wagner, 80–92 (Shippensburg, PA: Destiny Image, 2015). For more about dealing with external strongholds, see Derek Prince, *Pulling Down Strongholds* (New Kensington, PA: Whitaker House, 2013).

39. Crist, *Interceding*, 19.

others, you are called to bless those on the frontlines. Some battles are not to be fought at all. Knowing your role in each battle requires continual discernment.

Therefore, as we seek to strike the mark by hitting the right targets and recognizing false targets, the essential question becomes, "Who is leading you into this particular battle? The Lord or the enemy?" We are not called to follow the enemy; we are called to follow the Lamb of God wherever He goes. (See Revelation 14:4.) Yes, He always leads us into triumph. (See 2 Corinthians 2:14; Colossians 2:15.) Clearly, though, knowing where He is leading is the key! We must keep close to the Lord so we can hear what the Spirit is saying to us at each moment.

In the next chapter, we will build on this point as we explore further how to undergo progressive purification in preparation for being on the spiritual battlefield of intercessory prayer.

TARGET PRACTICE

Almighty God, I invite You to shine Your searchlight into my heart to reveal old darkness. I want to have no common ground with Satan and his demonic powers. Cleanse me with the blood of Jesus and make me whiter than snow. Help me to grow in wisdom and authority. Assist me as I align myself with Your Word, will, and ways so that I will grow in greater intimacy with Christ and become more effective in my role in spiritual warfare. Thank You for using me to displace the powers of darkness. In Jesus's name. Amen and amen!

10

THE GUARDIAN
OF INTERCESSION

*"He who dwells in the secret place of the Most High shall abide
under the shadow of the Almighty."*
—Psalm 91:1

As we learn how to move out in spiritual warfare on *all* levels, as the early Christians did, we must remember to maintain a balance between our upward reach (to God) and our outward reach (moving out into the world with His authority). If our outward reach exceeds our upward reach, we may get into big trouble.

The danger of going upward without going outward is simply ineffectiveness in ministry. Remember, *"faith without works is dead"* (James 2:26). However, the risk of going outward without going upward may be much more serious; truly, it is like making yourself a sheep among wolves. Combatting Satan is not a video war game. When intercessory prayer involves spiritual warfare, you must pay attention to what you are doing—for your own protection. Keep things in balance.

In the following diagram, the degree of "reach" is represented arbitrarily with numbers one through ten. The shaded area represents the danger zone.[40]

---

40. This diagram is based on one presented by C. Peter Wagner in chapter 6 of his book *Warfare Prayer: What the Bible Says About Spiritual Warfare.* (See footnote 16.)

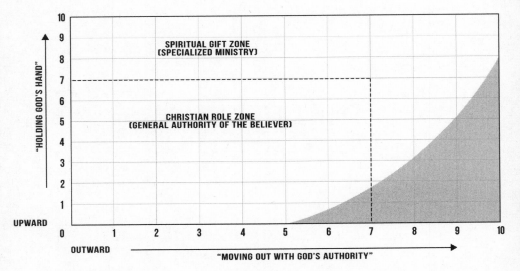

Every believer, regardless of gifting and maturity level, should be able to operate within what some refer to as the "Christian Role Zone" as they minister to others. Other believers, because of their God-given spiritual gifts and their active practice in using them, may be able to reach both higher and wider without suffering negative consequences. The only human being who could ever reach a ten on both scales would be Jesus Himself, and He did.

Years ago, in a vision, I saw this very chart as if it were projected onto a wall. Then, an umbrella appeared over the top of it, becoming like a shield over the upward-outward workings below it. (Specifically, the umbrella was one of those compact, travel umbrellas. This signified to me that the protection was meant for those who go "out there" in spiritual warfare intercession, like forerunners.) The Holy Spirit interpreted for me this vision of the umbrella and called it "the guardian of intercession" or "the protectorate," indicating that high-level intercessors needed such additional protection from spiritual storms.

This was a new way to picture a "prayer shield," or the concerted protective prayers we should pray for our brothers and sisters in Christ whose gifts propel them into the forefront of the spiritual battleground. If "*two are better than one*" (Ecclesiastes 4:9), what would it be like if there were ten, twenty, or thirty effective intercessors for every point person in the field? Instead of it being hell on earth, it could be heaven on earth! Let's aim high and ask the Lord for wisdom in our intercession.

Over the years, I have had various applications of prayer shields for my life, family, and ministry. At one point, I had the involvement of a thousand personal prayer warriors. Later, I learned that it could be as effective—or even more effective—if I had thirty mature personal intercessors who walked in unity together. I also learned that it was vital for me to be in regular communications with them, giving instruction and leading the charge by example.

E. M. Bounds, pastor, author, and prayer leader during the Civil War, taught his disciples to pray for their pastor. This dear man of God led a prayer revival at the Methodist church in downtown Franklin, Tennessee, for three straight years. We need more leaders like that today! Remember, praying for those in authority is essential, and every leader needs the umbrella of spiritual protection lifted high over their life.[41]

PREPARED FOR BATTLE

We have seen that before we move into our battle positions as spiritual warriors, we must first allow the Holy Spirit to purify us so that the enemy cannot infiltrate our thoughts and decisions. We need to fill ourselves with the truth of God's Word as part of our armament: *"Stand therefore, having girded your waist with truth, having put on the breastplate of righteousness"* (Ephesians 6:14).

New levels of light reveal old levels of darkness. Everything inside of us must go through progressive purification as a preparation for the spiritual battlefield of intercessory prayer. It is very much like what we read in the book of Numbers:

---

41. For more teaching on praying for those in authority and the importance of a prayer shield, see my book *Prayer Storm* (see footnote 4) and its companion book *Prayer Storm Study Guide: The Hour That Changes the World* (Shippensburg, PA: Destiny Image, 2008).

Then Eleazar the priest said to the soldiers who had gone into battle, "This is what is required by the law that the LORD gave Moses: Gold, silver, bronze, iron, tin, lead and anything else that can withstand fire must be put through the fire, and then it will be clean. But it must also be purified with the water of cleansing. And whatever cannot withstand fire must be put through that water."

(Numbers 31:21–23 NIV)

We must close any "back door" to the enemy that the Lord shows us, so that we can be as much like Jesus as possible—allowing ourselves no common ground with the evil one. (See John 14:30.) Let's read again what Terry Crist wrote concerning this: "When the devil struck at Jesus [as he did in the wilderness encounters], there was nothing whatsoever in Him to receive the 'hit.' When Satan examined Him, there was nothing [impure] for him to find. Jesus and Satan had no relationship one to another, no common ground. There was nothing in Jesus's life that could be aligned with darkness."[42] (By the way, when Jesus died on the cross, the enemy did not take His life. It was not the hits of the devil that killed Jesus, because He laid down His own life willingly and with the authority of the Father. See John 10:17–18.)

We must always avoid sinful behavior, because that is where we share common ground with the evil one. Jesus linked His betrayer Judas directly with Satan when He called him *"a devil"*: *"Jesus replied, 'Have I not chosen you, the Twelve? Yet one of you is a devil!' (He meant Judas, the son of Simon Iscariot, who, though one of the Twelve, was later to betray him.)"* (John 6:70–71 NIV). However, it does not have to be obvious sinful behavior, such as murder or fornication, to make us slip onto common ground with the enemy. Take something as seemingly harmless as grumbling or murmuring, for example. When Miriam and Aaron spoke against their brother Moses, the Lord was angry with them and seriously took them to task for their dissention, temporarily smiting Miriam with leprosy. (See Numbers 12.) Or how about underhanded thievery, for which the Israelite Achan was punished with death? (See Joshua 7.)

---

42. See footnote 39.

How can you escape the consequences once you have sinned? By remembering that you belong to Jesus, who died for your sins so that you could be set free. Therefore, when the Holy Spirit convicts you, do not try to hide behind excuses. Simply confess your sin and repent, asking God to forgive both your sinful actions and your wrong motives. Then ask God to help you change your behavior and tendencies. Continue to serve the Lord, immersing yourself in His Word and surrounding yourself with other believers who are serious about walking in righteousness.

I used to say that God was "the God of the second chance." I no longer make such overly simplistic statements. By the grace of God, I now declare that our God is the God of the fifty-millionth chance! God is for us, and He is always ready to bring us into renewed fellowship with Himself and to help restore us to our cutting edge.

As Terry Crist reminded us, perhaps one reason so many ministers and intercessors have been taken down by the fiery arrows of the enemy is that they had some hidden common ground with the enemy. Let's not be counted among them! Let's take every thought captive to Christ (see 2 Corinthians 10:5) and allow the Holy Spirit to purify us so that we will be ready for the battles ahead. Let wisdom be our guide!

God knows where He wants to position us. Remember—you will not have to fight in every battle and neither will I. God is in charge, and He always, always leads us in triumph: *"Thanks be to God, who always leads us in triumph in Christ, and manifests through us the sweet aroma of the knowledge of Him in every place"* (2 Corinthians 2:14 NASB).

GRADUATE COURSE: WILDERNESS TRAINING

As we progress in our faith and purification, we go from lessons to tests, from trials to triumphs, and *"from glory to glory"* (2 Corinthians 3:18). There are endless lessons and classes to take in the Holy Spirit's "Wisdom Academy." I am continually enrolled in the "School of the Holy Spirit." How about you?

Perhaps one of the graduate-level courses in God's wisdom and ways is called "How Do We Respond During Wilderness Times?"

Now, we all wish we had continuous mountaintop experiences. But let's be real—there are no mountains without the valleys in between. No valleys, no mountains. It is the same in the spiritual as it is in the natural.

So, what are some of the lessons we can apply when walking through a wilderness time in which we learn vital spiritual truths and undergo purification? Here are a few practical points with some supporting Scriptures:

1. When the Lord reveals aspects of your life that need to change, it is for the purpose of a reality check. How should you respond? Simply say, "Thank You, God, for showing me what was in my heart. Now let's do something about it!" (See Psalm 139:23–24.)

2. Repent, asking God to forgive any sin or even wrong motivations. You may need to ask others for forgiveness as well. (See Psalm 51:1–10.)

3. Seek God's help to overcome wrong motivations and sins, and to create godly habits and attitudes. (See Ephesians 3:16; 2 Peter 1:5–8.)

4. Resist the enemy in his attacks on your life. (See James 4:7.)

5. Never be in denial that you are going through a wilderness experience. (See 1 John 1:8–10.)

6. Never feel condemned for that which has surfaced during your wilderness journey. (See Romans 8:1–2.)

7. Keep trusting in God's process of purification as you continuously offer Him praise and thanksgiving. (See 1 Thessalonians 5:16–18, 23–24.)

Satan's condemnation paralyzes us because it tends to be rather general and vague. In contrast, the conviction of the Holy Spirit is specific and penetrates us deeply so it can be responded to immediately. The true conviction of the Spirit leads to freedom and not to long-term heaviness and bondage. Conviction is a tool of freedom. Condemnation is a tool of bondage.

CONCLUDING THOUGHTS

Let's commit to cooperating with God when He points out areas in our lives we need to change. That is the personal, endearing ministry of His Spirit, the Dove of God. Allow the Spirit's cleansing work to go deep so there will be less ground in our lives that has commonality with the devil and his dark domain. This work of sanctification is the path of walking in the protectorate of God, where we have ongoing victory over our internal and external enemies.

As we individually cooperate with God's progressive, sanctifying fires in our lives, we are supernaturally enabled by the power of the Holy Spirit to reach out in ministry to others. Let's seek to hold on to God's mighty hand, which, by grace, is already reaching out to us. With this kind of God-confidence and assurance of faith, we can launch prayers that strike the mark in the authority that Christ Jesus has already won on the cross.

Remember, *"the LORD is a man of war"* (Exodus 15:3). Our God is mighty within us! *"Greater is He who is in you than he who is in the world"* (1 John 4:4 NASB)! Yes and amen!

TARGET PRACTICE

Almighty God, I submit myself to Your purification process by the Holy Spirit so I can become more like You and prevent the enemy from infiltrating my thoughts and decisions. As part of my armament, I will fill myself with the truth of Your Word. I will also commit to helping form a prayer shield for leaders in the church whose gifts propel them into the forefront of spiritual battleground. Protect and keep them in Your care. Thank You for always leading us in triumph in Christ! In Jesus's name, amen.

11

THE POWER OF THE BLOOD

"You have come to Mount Zion and to the city of the living God,
the heavenly Jerusalem, and to myriads of angels,
to the general assembly and church of the firstborn who are
enrolled in heaven, and to God, the Judge of all,
and to the spirits of the righteous made perfect, and to Jesus,
the mediator of a new covenant, and to the sprinkled blood,
which speaks better than the blood of Abel."
—Hebrews 12:22–24 (NASB)

The above words give us a glimpse of heaven, where God surveys the souls of those who have been perfectly cleansed of their sin by the blood shed by His Son Jesus on the cross. His blood has done it all. Forevermore, it declares that restitution has been made for sin and that even the blackest heart can be made pure before the judgment seat of God.

Jesus's blood *"speaks better than the blood of Abel,"* which means it perpetually calls down justice and mercy from the throne of our almighty Father. We read in the fourth chapter of Genesis how Cain and Abel, the sons of Adam and Eve, were together in a field, and Cain killed Abel in a fit of jealousy. (See Genesis 4:1–8.) This is what happened next:

> *The* LORD *said to Cain, "Where is Abel your brother?" He said,*
> *"I do not know. Am I my brother's keeper?" And He said, "What*
> *have you done? The voice of your brother's blood cries out to Me*
> *from the ground."* (Genesis 4:9–10)

The blood-soaked earth was crying out for recompense, saying, "Do something! Punish this man for murdering his innocent brother!"

The blood cried out because of the following principle, which runs throughout Scripture: *"The life of the flesh is in the blood"* (Leviticus 17:11). Abel was innocent of wrongdoing, and that fact gave loud voice to the silent, red pool saturating the soil around his fatally injured body. As we discover when we read further, the Lord did punish Cain:

> *So now you are cursed from the earth, which has opened its mouth*
> *to receive your brother's blood from your hand. When you till the*
> *ground, it shall no longer yield its strength to you. A fugitive and a*
> *vagabond you shall be on the earth.* (Genesis 4:11–12)

Sin persisted in rampaging throughout the world. Over the passage of long years, Abel's innocent blood continued to cry out in vain wherever human sin did its dirty work. Nothing could permanently take away the stain of sin, certainly not eye-for-eye vengeance or the blood of animal sacrifices instituted under the law of Moses. Nothing sufficed until Jesus, the Son of God, the Lamb of God, came onto the scene. His bloody crucifixion paid the price for sin once and for all.

This is what Jesus wanted His disciples to understand at their last supper together before His arrest: *"And he took a cup of wine and gave thanks to God for it. He gave it to them, and they all drank from it. And he said to them, 'This is my blood, which confirms the covenant between God and his people. It is poured out as a sacrifice for many'"* (Mark 14:23–24 NLT).

Again, as the old gospel song declares, "Nothing but the blood of Jesus." Only Jesus's shed blood avails. Nothing else even comes close.

PLEADING THE BLOOD

As intercessors, when we stand in the gap in prayer for others, we "plead the blood" of Jesus before God's throne. This means we declare the truth of Christ's shed blood and apply it to the situation we are praying for. We state our faith in the superior power of the sacrificed blood of God's own Son to set right a particular wrong. We cry out for God's mercy, knowing that, because of His blood, *"mercy triumphs over judgment"* (James 2:13). When we pray like this, our prayers strike the mark without fail.

In this way, we remind God of His Word, a practice we learned about in chapter 4 of this book. However, we must first understand the benefits of the blood and the cross before we can apply them. The Word tells us what the blood of the Lamb has already accomplished. Therefore, we can make declarations, not only petitions; and at times, we move into spiritual warfare, putting on the armor of God and declaring to Satan what Jesus has accomplished.

We overcome Satan when we testify personally about what the Word of God says the blood of Christ does for us. (See Revelation 12:11.) Therefore, *"let the redeemed of the LORD say so, whom He has redeemed from the hand of the adversary"* (Psalm 107:2 NASB). In a sermon called "Pleading," famed preacher Charles Spurgeon said this:

> Do not reckon you have prayed unless you have pleaded, for pleading is the very marrow of prayer. He who pleads well knows the secret of prevailing with God, especially if he pleads the blood of Jesus, for that unlocks the treasury of heaven. Many keys fit many locks, but the master-key is the blood and the name of Him that died but rose again, and ever lives in heaven to save unto the uttermost.[43]

The most powerful plea before God, the devil, and the world is the blood of Jesus Christ. We have no merit of our own. We cannot prevail over evil by virtue of our prayer technique or life experience. We can only bring ourselves into God's presence because of the blood of His

---

43. The Spurgeon Archive, http://archive.spurgeon.org/sermons/1018.php.

Son Jesus, and we can only prevail over the forces of wickedness by means of that same blood. Yes, "there's power in the blood"!

CHRIST'S BLOOD SPRINKLED SEVEN TIMES

Before Jesus came to earth and established the new covenant with His blood, the old covenant priests made every effort to atone for the sins of the people. Once a year, on the Day of Atonement, the high priest, serving as the mediator between God and the people, would first minister at the altar of incense, and then, having sacrificed a bull followed by a goat, he would open the heavy veil and go into the Most Holy Place two times. There, he would take some of the animal blood and sprinkle it with his finger on the mercy seat and in front of the mercy seat, seven times each. (See, for example, Leviticus 16.)

Why seven times? In the Bible, seven is considered the number of completion. In particular, the creation is described in Genesis as occurring within seven days. Seven applications of the blood completed the act of atonement—at least until the next time.

The high priest went into the Holy of Holies only once a year, and he had to follow the ritual perfectly. There was no access into the presence of God without the shedding of sacrificial blood. Many people have found a strong connection between the sevenfold sprinkling of blood on the Day of Atonement and Jesus's shedding of blood on the cross—which achieved, on behalf of the people, perfect atonement with God.

On the Day of Atonement, the seven sprinklings of blood were applied in three places: on the mercy seat, in front of the mercy seat, and upon the horns of the brazen (bronze) altar. (See verses 14–15, 18–19.) Some Bible teachers see the number three as signifying the Godhead, or Trinity, and that, combined with the number of completion (seven), this was meant to be a picture of what was yet to come when Jesus, the ultimate High Priest, would shed His blood to atone for sins for all time.

The fundamental message is clear: there is no access to the presence of God without the shedding of sacrificial blood.

For over two thousand years, human sin has been covered by the blood of Christ. Ever since Jesus rose from the dead after His crucifixion, those who put their faith in Him receive the atoning benefits of His shed blood. And just as His sacrificial death was foreshadowed in the sevenfold rituals of the Day of Atonement, so the actual shedding of His blood follows a sevenfold pattern. With this in mind, let's review the crucifixion account.

1. SWEATING BLOOD

The night *before* the cross may have been even more agonizing for Jesus than actually being crucified. The act of deciding to accept the harrowing torture that would end in death—with full foreknowledge of what it would entail—was so grueling that blood actually exuded from the pores of Jesus's forehead: *"He was in such agony of spirit that he broke into a sweat of blood, with great drops falling to the ground as he prayed more and more earnestly"* (Luke 22:44 TLB). This is the initial blood-shedding of our Lord Jesus Christ. The Old Testament high priests had to slaughter bulls and goats to obtain the sacrificial blood, but Christ became the sacrificial Lamb, shedding His very own blood to atone for the sin of fallen humanity.

2. STRUCK AND BEATEN

Jesus was arrested in the middle of the night and taken forcibly from Gethsemane to the house of the high priest, Caiaphas, where the scribes and elders had assembled. There He was questioned and handled roughly:

The high priest stood up and said to Him, "Do You not answer? What is it that these men are testifying against You?" But Jesus kept silent. And the high priest said to Him, "I adjure You by the living God, that You tell us whether You are the Christ, the Son of God." Jesus said to him, "You have said it yourself; nevertheless I tell you, hereafter you will see the Son of Man sitting at the right hand of Power, and coming on the clouds of heaven." Then the high priest tore his robes and said, "He has blasphemed! What further need do we have of witnesses? Behold, you have now heard the blasphemy; what do you think?" They answered, "He deserves death!" Then they spat in His face and beat Him with their fists [or with rods]; and others slapped Him.

(Matthew 26:62–67 NASB)

Surely, this beating drew blood, although it was nothing like the scourging that was to follow.

3. BEARD PLUCKED OUT

In biblical times, if you wanted to express utter abhorrence and dishonor toward a man, you would not only beat him and slap his face, but you would also spit in his face and tear out his beard. This would get ugly, undoubtedly, because as each chunk of beard was ripped out, it would take a piece of the flesh of the man's cheek or chin with it. We believe that this form of dishonor happened to Jesus because the prophet Isaiah foretold it: *"I gave My back to those who struck Me, and My cheeks to those who plucked out the beard; I did not hide My face from shame and spitting"* (Isaiah 50:6).

This third aspect of the bloody crucifixion ordeal is often left out of contemporary renderings of the story, as it is not specifically recorded in the gospel accounts. I have had some form of a beard for over forty-five years, and I cannot imagine how painful it would be to have my beard torn off my face. No wonder Isaiah spoke of the Messiah's appearance as being *"marred"* (Isaiah 52:14), or *"disfigured"* (TLB, NLT) beyond recognition.

4. BACK SCOURGED

The above prophetic passage from Isaiah says, *"I gave My back to those who struck Me"* (Isaiah 50:6), and this also happened to Jesus before His death: *"And all the people answered and said, 'His blood be on us and on our children.' Then he [Pilate] released Barabbas to them; and when he had scourged Jesus, he delivered Him to be crucified"* (Matthew 27:25–26). To be scourged under the Roman system was a brutal punishment, sometimes resulting in the death of the one who had been whipped: "The punishment of scourging was common among the

Jews.... Under the Roman method the culprit was stripped, stretched with cords or thongs on a frame and beaten with rods. (Another form of the scourge consisted of a handle with three lashes or thongs of leather or cord, sometimes with pieces of metal fastened to them.)"[44]

The defenseless prisoner would be flayed alive until bloody strips of flesh and muscle were hanging from his back. Do you get the picture? Not only would Jesus's face no longer have been recognizable, but also, His back would have been plowed open. I do not want to imagine this scene! For love's sake, our Lord Jesus endured this fourth profuse blood-shedding.

5. HEAD PIERCED WITH CROWN OF THORNS

Jesus's precious blood was shed in a fifth way when the Roman soldiers plaited a mock crown from thorny branches and pressed it into His scalp, causing the blood to run down over His face: "*And they stripped Him and put a scarlet robe on Him. When they had twisted a crown of thorns, they put it on His head, and a reed in His right hand. And they bowed the knee before Him and mocked Him*" (Matthew 27:28–29). The thorns pierced His skin like sharp needles, penetrating down to the bone of His skull.

6. CRUCIFIED

Bleeding profusely, Jesus was forced to carry His own cross through the streets to the site of crucifixion. There, spikes were driven into His wrists and feet to attach Him to the rough wood of the cross. (See Matthew 27:35; Mark 15:22–24; Luke 23:32–33; 24:38–40; John 19:18.) This was at least the sixth time that Jesus, the sacrificial Lamb, willingly spilled His blood.

Oh, how deep and wide was the love of God demonstrated when the hammer fell on the nails driven through the wrists and feet of the only Son of God! Suffering the cruel death of crucifixion, this one sinless Man was penalized by being executed like a criminal.

---

44. M. G. Easton, M.A., D.D., "Scourging," *Illustrated Bible Dictionary*, 3rd. ed. (New York: T. Nelson and Sons, 1897).

7. SIDE PIERCED

Even after His death, Jesus's blood was shed once more: *"One of the soldiers pierced His side with a spear, and immediately blood and water came out"* (John 19:34).

Seven times, the innocent blood of the Lamb of God was shed so that you and I could be freed from our slavery to sin and certain death.

CHRIST'S BLOOD AVAILS

In the Scriptures, we can find many benefits concerning what the blood of Jesus has done for us. We overcome the devil and his works when we testify to what Jesus's blood has accomplished. We become like those believers who are already in heaven, having followed Him faithfully all the way: *"They triumphed over him by the blood of the Lamb and by the word of their testimony; they did not love their lives so much as to shrink from death"* (Revelation 12:11 NIV). Jesus's triumph over the powers of darkness is reinforced whenever we agree with and declare the benefits of His precious shed blood.

In Christ's blood, we receive life that death cannot conquer. (See, for example, Isaiah 53:12; John 6:53–57; Hebrews 12:24.) Jesus has established a new covenant through His blood, and He intercedes on our behalf to enable us to enter more fully into His blood covenant with us. (See Romans 8:34.)

SEVEN BENEFITS OF JESUS'S SHED BLOOD

Once again, the number seven comes into play as Jesus's blood accomplishes at least seven distinct benefits to complete our salvation:

1. *Forgiveness.* You and I have been forgiven through the blood that Jesus shed when He gave up His life. *"Without shedding of blood there is no forgiveness"* (Hebrews 9:22 NASB). For this reason, confidence, peace, and joy can now replace condemnation, anxiety, and grief in our lives.

2. *Cleansing.* Our consciences have been washed by the blood of Christ Jesus because we have truly been purified from all sin. (See

Hebrews 9:14.) *"But if we walk in the Light as He Himself is in the Light, we have fellowship with one another, and the blood of Jesus His Son cleanses us from all sin"* (1 John 1:7 NASB).

3. *Redemption.* Forgiven and cleansed, we find that we have been redeemed from the clutches of the powers of darkness. We are no longer forced to live in the dark, because we have been transferred into the kingdom of light (see Colossians 1:12–13 NIV, TLB), where the beloved Son of God appears in glory:

> *In him we have redemption through his blood, the forgiveness of sins, in accordance with the riches of God's grace.*
>
> (Ephesians 1:7 NIV)

> *God paid a ransom to save you from the impossible road to heaven which your fathers tried to take, and the ransom he paid was not mere gold or silver as you very well know. But he paid for you with the precious lifeblood of Christ, the sinless, spotless Lamb of God.*
>
> (1 Peter 1:18–19 TLB)

4. *Justification.* It is one thing to believe that you are forgiven, cleansed, and redeemed, but it is another to believe that it is just as if you had never sinned in the first place. *"For He made Him who knew no sin to be sin for us, that we might become the righteousness of God in Him"* (2 Corinthians 5:21). When I am justified, it is "just as if I'd" never sinned. I am righteous. I now belong to the King and have obtained citizenship in His kingdom. I have a fresh passport that says, "Citizen of the Kingdom of Heaven."

5. *Sanctification.* Now we can take it one step further and declare that we have been set apart for a holy calling—sanctified. Each believer is a special vessel set apart for God. Only Jesus's blood can make this possible. Because of Him, we can walk on the straight and narrow way. (See Matthew 7:14.) *"Make straight paths for your feet, so that the limb which is lame may not be put out of joint, but rather be healed"* (Hebrews 12:13 NASB).

6. *Peace.* Because of Jesus's blood, we can have perfect peace. There will still be plenty of battles to fight, but the outcome has been determined on Calvary: *"It was through what his Son did that God cleared a path for everything to come to him—all things in heaven and on earth—for Christ's death on the cross has made peace with God for all by his blood"* (Colossians 1:20 TLB).

7. *Access to the throne.* Jesus's blood has made possible your complete reconciliation with the Holy Father in heaven. Now, covered as you are in the blood of Christ, you are like the high priest who was invited to enter the Most Holy Place—without being struck dead. You can enter the most holy throne room of heaven with perfect impunity: *"And so, dear brothers, now we may walk right into the very Holy of Holies, where God is, because of the blood of Jesus"* (Hebrews 10:19 TLB).

Because of what Jesus accomplished on the cross, we have all this, and heaven besides!

In your own life, how have you testified to what the blood of Jesus Christ has accomplished? How have you spoken of it (out loud) and declared with joy the benefits He has won for you? Even when you proclaim it within the privacy of your prayer closet, the enemy gets blinded with the glory of heaven!

All praise, honor, and worship to the Lamb of God for what He has done on the cross! The blood of Christ avails for you and for me!

TARGET PRACTICE

Pray and proclaim this prayer about the power of Christ's blood, which I was taught by Derek Prince. Pray it for yourself and for others:

Through the blood of Jesus, I am redeemed out of the hand
of the devil.
Through the blood of Jesus, all my sins are forgiven.
The blood of Jesus Christ, God's Son, continually cleanses
me from all sin.
Through the blood of Jesus, I am justified, made righteous,
just-as-if-I'd never sinned.

Through the blood of Jesus, I am sanctified, made holy, set
apart to God.

My body is a temple of the Holy Spirit, redeemed, cleansed
by the blood of Jesus.

Satan has no place in me, no power over me, through the
blood of Jesus! Amen.[45]

---

45. See also Derek Prince, *Prayers and Proclamations* (New Kensington, PA: Whitaker House, 2010), 163–164.

12

PRAYING FROM A VICTORIOUS PERSPECTIVE

"Oh, sing to the LORD a new song! For He has done marvelous things; His right hand and His holy arm have gained Him the victory. The LORD has made known His salvation; His righteousness He has revealed in the sight of the nations. He has remembered His mercy and His faithfulness to the house of Israel; all the ends of the earth have seen the salvation of our God. Shout joyfully to the LORD, all the earth; break forth in song, rejoice, and sing praises.... Shout joyfully before the LORD, the King. Let the sea roar, and all its fullness, the world and those who dwell in it."
—Psalm 98:1–4, 6–7

You are not a loser. I am not a loser. None of us who belong to Jesus are losers. Although we may wear out our knees praying and shed passionate, desperate tears, all of our prayers that strike the mark are winning prayers—prayers of victory.

I want you to know that I am still learning the lessons contained in this chapter. The following principle and revelation continues to seep down into my soul: We do not labor *toward* victory but *from* victory. In all reality, this one truth affects every aspect of my Christian life—especially my prayer life!

Yes, the One to whom we pray has already won the spiritual battle once and for all. Jesus is the Victor! As long as we are on this earth, we will have a vital role to play—to help enforce the victory of Calvary—but we do not have to worry about the final outcome, because it was already decided a long time ago when Jesus, nailed to the blood-soaked cross, declared, "*It is finished!*" (John 19:30). Those three words resound across the universe and down the epochs of time. Jesus's death and subsequent miraculous resurrection secured and sealed the victory over the darkness of rebellion and sin forevermore.

PROCLAMATIONS OF VICTORY

For each of us, life will involve many ups and downs, trials and tribulations, winds and waves. This is the normal Christian life: "*We must go through many hardships to enter the kingdom of God*" (Acts 14:22 NIV). In God's economy, our hardships work for us, not against us: "*Rejoice inasmuch as you participate in the sufferings of Christ, so that you may be overjoyed when his glory is revealed*" (1 Peter 4:13 NIV). But this does not mean that the outcome is up for grabs; and for sure, it does not depend on our own strength.

Christ's victory: this is the perspective from which we must live and pray.

This perspective keeps our prayers from falling to the ground before they strike their intended target. It makes many of our prayers sound more like *proclamations* than humble pleading. Like court heralds, we proclaim God's sovereign greatness and we announce good news. (Well, it is bad news to the demonic forces over whom Jesus has won the victory.)

Proclamations of God's victory are powerful, and that is why we find them throughout the Scriptures. Just like those who penned such proclamations, we must align our hearts with God's heart of victory, expressing our trust in His fatherly oversight even when the way ahead looks dark and foreboding.

The kingdom of God is speech-activated. As we store up His Word in our hearts, we have an abundance of truth to proclaim with our mouths. Even in the face of fear, we can speak from faith. We can proclaim, "Freedom!" in places where nobody knows the meaning of the word anymore. We can proclaim God's extravagant mercy from the rooftops, declaring His lordship over our cities and their people. Jesus told His disciples, *"What I tell you now in the darkness, shout abroad when daybreak comes. What I whisper in your ear, shout from the housetops for all to hear!"* (Matthew 10:27 NLT).

PROCLAMATIONS OF PRAISE

Purposefully, the writers of Scripture frequently proclaim God's greatness. Putting aside their needs and requests, they simply praise Him for His own sake:

> *I will proclaim the name of the LORD; how glorious is our God! He is the Rock; his deeds are perfect. Everything he does is just and fair. He is a faithful God who does no wrong; how just and upright he is!* (Deuteronomy 32:3–4 NLT)

Praise is a sacrifice as well as a joyful sound, because it will cost you something. *"With Jesus' help we will continually offer our sacrifice of praise to God by telling others of the glory of his name"* (Hebrews 13:15 TLB). The sacrifice of praise is worth it—always—because praise is a spiritual warfare weapon, a means of deliverance from the strongholds of darkness. *"He who offers a sacrifice of thanksgiving honors Me; and to him who orders his way aright I shall show the salvation of God"* (Psalm 50:23 NASB). Sometimes we simply need to praise our way out of the entrapment of the enemy by releasing the high praise of God from our hearts—out loud. (One of the reasons it is good to store up the Word of God in our hearts is so that our high praises have something to flow from.)

> *The Lord declares that the happy voices of bridegrooms and of brides and the joyous song of those bringing thanksgiving offerings to the Lord will be heard again in this doomed land. The people will sing: "Praise the Lord! For he is good and his mercy endures*

forever!" For I will make this land happier and more prosperous than it has ever been before. (Jeremiah 33:10–11 TLB)

Praise is like a mantle—we can choose to put it on like clothing. And when we begin to praise the Lord, heaviness of spirit disappears. We look different, act different, and talk different when we put on a *"garment of praise"*!

The Spirit of the Sovereign Lord *is on me, because the* Lord *has anointed me to proclaim good news to the poor. He has sent me to bind up the brokenhearted, to proclaim freedom for the captives and release from darkness for the prisoners, to proclaim the year of the* Lord's *favor and the day of vengeance of our God, to comfort all who mourn, and provide for those who grieve in Zion—to bestow on them a crown of beauty instead of ashes, the oil of joy instead of mourning, and a garment of praise instead of a spirit of despair.* (Isaiah 61:1–3 NIV)

At times, we must toss off our dignity and, like children, give expression to radical praise for the Lord. This type of praise will silence Satan and halt his works in their tracks. The psalmist wrote, *"Out of the mouth of babes and nursing infants You have ordained strength, because of Your enemies, that You may silence the enemy and the avenger"* (Psalm 8:2)—and Jesus quoted this verse (see Matthew 21:15–16).

Often, we praise God in the dark, and our efforts can be a true sacrifice. We may be discouraged and weak, buffeted by adversities of all kinds. However, one of the best times to praise the Lord is when you feel the worst. By opening your mouth in praise, you come into His throne room. *"[God,] You are holy, enthroned in the praises of Israel"* (Psalm 22:3).

Praising God's greatness shifts the atmosphere into one of victory. The proclamation of praise establishes a highway from God's throne to earth and makes possible a visitation of His presence. As we glorify and praise the Lord, He returns our praises to us in the form of blessings.

THE POWER OF PROCLAMATION

When the prophet Jonah was at his lowest point after being swallowed by a large fish, it was not until he offered up a sacrifice of praise that God delivered him, causing the fish to vomit him up. This resulted not only in Jonah's deliverance, but also in revival for the populous city of Nineveh. (See Jonah 2–3.) What do you usually do when you are at a low point? That is exactly the time you need to shift into the power of proclamation.

In the New Testament, we read about how Paul and Silas were set free supernaturally from their prison cell as they declared vibrant praise to the Lord—after which their jailor and his whole family came to faith in Christ. (See Acts 16:22–34.) We can break the bars of the evil one when, in our darkest moments and darkest places, we proclaim the majesty of His great name.

As we talked about in the previous chapter, we need to proclaim the power of the shed blood of Christ Jesus. We apply it to our minds and hearts for cleansing from dead works (see Hebrews 9:14) and from distortions of truth sent by the accuser of the brethren (Satan). On occasion, we find that our consistent proclamation of Christ's blood finds verification in unusual ways.

One time, after my wife had died and I was alone in my home, suffering from a lot of physical weakness and pain, I had to call a friend of mine to take me to the emergency room. I felt so ill I thought my internal organs were shutting down. I had already been through three bouts of cancer and other ailments, and I had been treated with some wickedly powerful drugs, so it could have been anything this time. They put me on an IV right away in case I was dehydrated, and they began to run tests. They did extensive blood work and ordered a scan of my internal organs. Four and a half hours later, the doctor came back into my room and said, "We could not find anything wrong. Your blood work is perfect."

I asked him to explain that statement in detail. It seemed as if my blood work should show *some* problem. I asked him to spell out the test results in detail. So, he went through every line and it was all perfect, even my cholesterol. And the scan had showed nothing wrong with my internal organs. The doctor took my hand and said, "Whatever you are doing, you are doing something right; keep it up."

My friend and I were shaking our heads. I still felt terrible, and my legs were like wet noodles. But, you know, I have the blood of the Lamb flowing through my blood. There is life in the blood, and the blood of the Lamb is victorious. I may not have felt restored yet in my outer weakness, and I do not even now. But when I thought I was not going to make it, Jesus was showing me that His strength would be sufficient for me. (See 2 Corinthians 12:9.) And that is something to shout about! Even in the middle of the night, I will keep praising Him. Even when I can hardly walk and I am too feeble to raise both hands at the same time, I will still offer Him my sacrifice of praise, declaring the victory won by His shed blood.

Proclamation carries power—even when the hearers are hostile. Jesus proclaimed the truth of redemption every time He declared, ascribed, released, and pronounced light to both the Jews and the Gentiles. Paul proclaimed the truth of the gospel when he was arrested and taken before King Agrippa. Even as he stood before the stony-faced authorities, he turned his legal defense into a testimony, a proclamation about Jesus:

> *But God has protected me right up to this present time so I can testify to everyone, from the least to the greatest. I teach nothing except what the prophets and Moses said would happen—that the Messiah would suffer and be the first to rise from the dead, and in this way announce God's light to Jews and Gentiles alike.*
>
> (Acts 26:22–23 NLT)

The power of proclamation includes the power of preaching. In essence, we preach every time we proclaim to others what we have seen and heard so that they, also, may have intimate fellowship with the Father, Son, and Holy Spirit. The proclamation of the word of life is all-important to the salvation of others. The apostle John wrote:

We proclaim to you the one who existed from the beginning, whom we have heard and seen. We saw him with our own eyes and touched him with our own hands. He is the Word of life. This one who is life itself was revealed to us, and we have seen him. And now we testify and proclaim to you that he is the one who is eternal life. He was with the Father, and then he was revealed to us. We proclaim to you what we ourselves have actually seen and heard so that you may have fellowship with us. And our fellowship is with the Father and with his Son, Jesus Christ.   (1 John 1:1–3 NLT)

We must always be prepared to declare a prayerful proclamation of blessing. Such proclamations can take many forms, depending upon the people involved. Here are some examples:

1. A proclamation from the leaders to the people: *"May the LORD bless you and protect you. May the LORD smile on you and be gracious to you. May the LORD show you his favor and give you his peace"* (Numbers 6:24–26 NLT).

2. A proclamation from the people to the leaders: *"Finally, my brethren, be strong in the Lord and in the power of His might. Put on the whole armor of God, that you may be able to stand against the wiles of the devil.... [Pray] always with all prayer and supplication in the Spirit, being watchful to this end with all perseverance and supplication for all the saints"* (Ephesians 6:10–11, 18).

3. A proclamation over your family: *"As for me and my family, we will serve the Lord"* (Joshua 24:15 TLB).

4. A proclamation over your city: *"The earth is the LORD's, and all it contains, the world, and those who dwell in it.... Lift up your heads, O gates, and lift them up, O ancient doors, that the King of glory may come in!"* (Psalm 24:1, 9 NASB).

5. A proclamation over Israel: *"'The days are coming,' declares the LORD, 'when I will bring my people Israel and Judah back from captivity and restore them to the land I gave their ancestors to possess,' says the LORD"* (Jeremiah 30:3 NIV).

"DECREE A THING, AND IT WILL BE ESTABLISHED FOR YOU"

The Lord spoke to Job through his friend's counsel, and his words hold true for us today:

> *Yield now and be at peace with Him; thereby good will come to you. Please receive instruction from His mouth and establish His words in your heart. If you return to the Almighty, you will be restored; if you remove unrighteousness far from your tent, and place your gold in the dust, and the gold of Ophir among the stones of the brooks, then the Almighty will be your gold and choice silver to you. For then you will delight in the Almighty and lift up your face to God. You will pray to Him, and He will hear you; and you will pay your vows. You will also decree a thing, and it will be established for you; and light will shine on your ways.*
>
> (Job 22:21–28 NASB)

Conditions must be met—this could be called "process praying"—and then you reach a place where you can *"decree* [proclaim] *a thing"* and your prayers will reach their intended target without fail. If you proceed through the process below, your heart will be so well-primed that the decree will almost explode out of it.

The counsel given to Job essentially lays out these progressive conditions.

1. Confession of sin
2. Removal of obstacles that are in the way
3. Establishment of the Word of God in your heart
4. Having a heart of humble submission
5. Being willing to receive instruction (being "teachable")
6. Repentance and returning to the Lord
7. Receiving the revelation that God is your all
8. Removing other gods from your life
9. Making God your delight
10. Praying to the Lord

The result of this process is that *"you will also decree a thing, and it will be established for you."* Now, people have been known to take this promise out of context. Not bothering about the conditions, they make bold statements and expect to see results. For them, the promise becomes like a rabbit's foot or lucky charm. Their prayers are shallow.

But if you pay the price of meeting the conditions, you will be able to effectively make a decree. Notice that it does not say, *"God* will decree a thing." You will do it yourself, with your own mouth and by your own faith. This is not too much to expect for someone who is sold out to God. In fact, it is part of your birthright.

PRAYERS THAT STRIKE THE MARK!

Thus, we praise God and exalt His strength—and we remind Him of His promises. Tirelessly and persistently, we petition Him. By entering into His presence through our praises and reminding everyone within earshot (including ourselves) of His powerful benevolence, we shift into asking Him for what we need. Because we are praying with a heavenly perspective, enforcing the victory won by Christ's shed blood, we are enabled to intercede and pray prayers that strike the mark.

From a position of victory, we pray prayers of victory. We proclaim the all-sufficiency of our God and we draw heaven's blessings down to earth, saying, *"Your kingdom come. Your will be done on earth as it is in heaven"* (Matthew 6:10). We pray expecting God and His angels to break up the darkness with the brilliant light of His glory. *"For God, who said, 'Let light shine out of darkness,' made his light shine in our hearts to give us the light of the knowledge of God's glory displayed in the face of Christ"* (2 Corinthians 4:6 NIV).

Do we see His glory every time? No. Often, we pray in the dark. But we keep on praying because He has furnished us with indomitable faith. *"Arise, shine, for your light has come, and the glory of the LORD rises upon you. See, darkness covers the earth and thick darkness is over the peoples, but the LORD rises upon you and his glory appears over you"* (Isaiah 60:1–2 NIV).

Eventually, our prayers shift again. I can't tell you how this happens or how quickly it will occur. All I know is that there comes a time when you actually stop asking. This is because of an almost fierce and well-won peace that, even when the darkness still seems to prevail, makes you sure that your prayers have been heard and that God's best answers are bound for their destination. You start to thank Him and praise Him for the provision that may not yet be visible, confident that in due time, it will become manifest.

At that point, all you can do is praise Him anew, and you do. Your prayers are striking the mark!

TARGET PRACTICE

Proclaiming and declaring what Jesus has accomplished on the cross, I renew my praises for You, my King. I love You, Lord, and I want Your light to shine in me and through me. Have Your way, Lord. I declare that there is no lack in heaven and I call forth heaven to earth. Your kingdom come; Your will be done—right where I am, here on earth.

I join my prayers with others so that Your glory will strike the mark. Always in the invincible name of Jesus, with a big *amen!*

PRAYER RESOURCES

SCRIPTURAL PRAYERS AND BLESSINGS

Here are "ready-to-pray" prayers and blessings, most from the first-century church and from Jesus Himself, along with some from the Old Testament. This prayer resource and the two that follow were inspired during the years when I was on staff with Mike Bickle at the Grace Training Center (which preceded the International House of Prayer) in Kansas City. The imprint of Mike's thorough, systematic presentation style shows throughout these resources.

PRAY FOR THE SALVATION OF SINNERS:

+ For the Word to increase and to conquer opposition. (See 2 Thessalonians 3:1–2; Acts 13:12, 48; Psalm 2:8–9.)

+ For an open door to the gospel. (See Colossians 4:3–4.)

+ For the salvation of sinners. (See Romans 10:1.)

+ For every knee to bow before the Lord. (See Isaiah 45:22–25; Romans 14:11.)

+ For laborers anointed with power and conviction. (See Matthew 5:16; 9:37–38; Luke 10:2.)

+ For the exaltation of God. (See Psalm 110:1–7.)

+ For faith in the promises of God regarding salvation. (See 2 Peter 3:9.)

+ For God to grant people repentance. (See 2 Timothy 2:25–26.)

Turn to me and be saved, all you ends of the earth; for I am God, and there is no other. By myself I have sworn, my mouth has uttered in all integrity a word that will not be revoked: Before me every knee will bow; by me every tongue will swear. They will say of me, 'In the LORD alone are deliverance and strength.'" All who have raged against him will come to him and be put to shame. But all the descendants of Israel will find deliverance in the Lord and will make their boast in him.   (Isaiah 45:22–25 NIV)

Ask of Me, and I will give You the nations for Your inheritance, and the ends of the earth for Your possession. You shall break them with a rod of iron; you shall dash them to pieces like a potter's vessel.   (Psalm 2:8–9)

_____

_____

_____

_____

_____

_____

PRAY FOR THE RELEASE OF THE GIFTS, FRUIT, AND WISDOM OF THE HOLY SPIRIT TO THE CORPORATE BODY OF CHRIST:

+ For the spirit of wisdom and revelation; for true hope; for a full appreciation of the riches of the glorious inheritance of God. (See Ephesians 1:16–21.)

+ For God's will to be made known; for the release of conviction, gifts, and wisdom. (See Colossians 1:9–11; 4:12; James 1:5.)

+ For the release of the gifts of the Holy Spirit; wisdom; conviction; the fullness of God's love; and strength in the inner man. (See Ephesians 3:16–19, 2 Thessalonians 3:5.)

+ For growth in love and discernment and the fruit of righteousness. (See Philippians 1:9–11; 1 Thessalonians 3:12; 2 Thessalonians 3:5.)

+ For the church to be established, confirmed, restored, and made complete by the growth of wisdom, gifts, and holiness. (See 1 Thessalonians 3:10; 2 Corinthians 13:9; Hebrews 13:20–21; 1 Corinthians 1:8.)

+ For unity in the church, particularly for leaders. (See Romans 15:5–6; John 17:20–22.)

+ For comfort, grace, strength, peace, joy, and hope. (See 2 Thessalonians 2:16–17; 3:16; Romans 15:13.)

+ For grace, peace, joy, and victory over Satan. (See Romans 16:19–20; John 17:11–15.)

+ For the release of boldness to the saints of God. (See Acts 4:29–30; Ephesians 6:18–19.)

+ For purity, love, knowledge, discernment, and sanctification. (See 2 Corinthians 13:7–9; 1 Thessalonians 3:11–13; 5:23; John 17:11–17; Philippians 1:9.)

+ For anointed laborers for the harvest. (See Matthew 9:37–38; Luke 10:2.)

+ For the increase of the Word through wisdom and conviction, and for protection. (See 2 Thessalonians 3:1–2.)

- For an open door for the gospel. (See Colossians 4:3–4.)

- For grace and maturity for the body of Christ. (See 2 Thessalonians 1:11–12.)

- For a revelation of God's power and love. (See Ephesians 3:18–19; 2 Thessalonians 3:5.)

- For growth in patience, endurance, and steadfastness. (See Colossians 1:9, 11; 2 Thessalonians 3:5.)

I have not stopped thanking God for you. I pray for you constantly, asking God, the glorious Father of our Lord Jesus Christ, to give you spiritual wisdom and insight so that you might grow in your knowledge of God. I pray that your hearts will be flooded with light so that you can understand the confident hope he has given to those he called—his holy people who are his rich and glorious inheritance. I also pray that you will understand the incredible greatness of God's power for us who believe him. This is the same mighty power that raised Christ from the dead and seated him in the place of honor at God's right hand in the heavenly realms. Now he is far above any ruler or authority or power or leader or anything else—not only in this world but also in the world to come.

(Ephesians 1:16–21 NLT)

He said to his disciples, "The harvest is great, but the workers are few. So pray to the Lord who is in charge of the harvest; ask him to send more workers into his fields."   (Matthew 9:37–38 NLT)

Now may the God of peace who brought up our Lord Jesus from the dead, that great Shepherd of the sheep, through the blood of the everlasting covenant, make you complete in every good work to do His will, working in you what is well pleasing in His sight, through Jesus Christ, to whom be glory forever and ever. Amen.

(Hebrews 13:20–21)

PRAY FOR INDIVIDUALS, ESPECIALLY FOR TRAVELING MINISTERS OF THE GOSPEL:

+ Exhortations to pray for others. (See 2 Corinthians 1:11; 1 Thessalonians 5:25; Hebrews 13:18; Ephesians 6:18.)

+ For protection. (See Romans 15:30–31; 2 Thessalonians 3:1–2; Philemon 22; Acts 12:5, 12.)

+ For anointing (the door of power). (See Colossians 4:3.)

+ For wisdom. (See Proverbs 2:1–8.)

+ For deliverance from temptations and evil. (See Matthew 6:13; Luke 22:31–32; 2 Corinthians 13:7; Philippians 1:19.)

+ For peace of heart and mind. (See Philippians 4:7, 19.)

+ For boldness and inspiration. (See Ephesians 6:19.)

+ For the Word to spread. (See 2 Thessalonians 3:1.)

+ For mercy. (See 2 Timothy 1:16–18.)

+ For healing in time of sickness. (See James 5:14–15.)

+ For physical provision. (See Matthew 6:11.)

+ For justice and reparation of wrongs. (See 2 Timothy 4:14–15.)

+ For forgiveness. (See Matthew 6:12.)

Every young man who listens to me and obeys my instructions will be given wisdom and good sense. Yes, if you want better insight and discernment, and are searching for them as you would for lost money or hidden treasure, then wisdom will be given you and knowledge of God himself; you will soon learn the importance of reverence for the Lord and of trusting him. For the Lord grants wisdom! His every word is a treasure of knowledge and understanding. He grants good sense to the godly—his saints. He is their shield, protecting them and guarding their pathway.

(Proverbs 2:1–8 TLB)

_____

_____

_____

_____

_____

_____

PRAY FOR ISRAEL:

- For the salvation and restoration of the people of Israel. (See Romans 10:1; 11:26–27; Jeremiah 31:7; Psalm 80.)

- For the Lord to complete His work, saving and raising up Israel. (See Isaiah 62:6–7.)

- For deliverance, restitution, and liberation. (See Psalm 79; Psalm 83; Ezekiel 36:22–37.)

- For favor, revival, righteousness, and peace. (See Psalm 85.)

- For mercy, grace, and love. (See Psalm 86.)

- For Jerusalem (peace and prosperity). (See Psalm 122:6–7.)

Therefore say to the people of Israel, 'The Lord God says: I am bringing you back again, but not because you deserve it; I am doing it to protect my holy name, which you tarnished among the nations. I will honor my great name, that you defiled, and the people of the world shall know I am the Lord. I will be honored before their eyes by delivering you from exile among them. For I will bring you back home again to the land of Israel. "'*Then it will be as though I had sprinkled clean water on you, for you will be clean—your filthiness will be washed away, your idol worship gone. And I will give you a new heart—I will give you new and right desires—and put a new spirit within you. I will take out your stony hearts of sin and give you new hearts of love. And I will put my Spirit within you so that you will obey my laws and do whatever I command.* "'*And you shall live in Israel, the land which I gave your fathers long ago. And you shall be my people, and I will be your God. I will cleanse away your sins. I will abolish crop failures and famine. I will give you huge harvests from your fruit trees and fields, and never again will the surrounding nations be able to scoff at your land for its famines. Then you will remember your past sins and loathe yourselves for all the evils you did. But always remember this: It is not for your own sakes that I will do this, but for mine. O my people Israel, be utterly ashamed of all that you have done!'*" *The Lord God says: "When I cleanse you from your sins, I will bring you home again to Israel, and rebuild the ruins. Acreage will be cultivated again that through the years of exile lay empty as a barren wilderness; all who passed by were shocked to see the extent of ruin in your land. But when I bring you back, they will say, 'This God-forsaken land has become like Eden's garden! The ruined cities are rebuilt and walled and filled with people!' Then the nations all around—all those still left—will know that I, the Lord, rebuilt the ruins and planted lush crops in the wilderness. For I, the Lord, have promised it, and I will do it." The Lord God says: "I am ready to hear Israel's prayers for these blessings and to grant them their requests. Let them but ask, and I will multiply them like the flocks that fill Jerusalem's streets at the time of sacrifice. The ruined cities will be crowded once more, and everyone will know I am the Lord."*

(Ezekiel 36:33–38 TLB)

_____

_____

_____

_____

_____

PRAY FOR THOSE IN SECULAR AUTHORITY:

I urge, then, first of all, that petitions, prayers, intercession and thanksgiving be made for all people—for kings and all those in authority, that we may live peaceful and quiet lives in all godliness and holiness. This is good, and pleases God our Savior, who wants all people to be saved and to come to a knowledge of the truth. For there is one God and one mediator between God and mankind, the man Christ Jesus, who gave himself as a ransom for all people.

(1 Timothy 2:1–6 NIV)

Then if my people who are called by my name will humble themselves and pray and seek my face and turn from their wicked ways, I will hear from heaven and will forgive their sins and restore their land. (2 Chronicles 7:14 NLT)

Seek the peace of the city where I have caused you to be carried away captive, and pray to the LORD for it; for in its peace you will have peace. (Jeremiah 29:7)

_____

_____

_____

_____

_____

_____

PRAY FOR DELIVERANCE FROM PERSECUTION:

+ For deliverance from harm and a clean heart. (See Psalm 7.)
+ For vindication and restitution. (See Revelation 6:10; Psalm 55; 58; 59.)
+ For rescue and justice. (See Psalm 54; Psalm 94; Psalm 109.)
+ For mercy. (See Psalm 57; Habakkuk 3:2; Nehemiah 1:4–11.)
+ For hope and trust in God. (See Psalm 56.)

O LORD my God, in You I have taken refuge; save me from all those who pursue me, and deliver me, or he will tear my soul like a lion, dragging me away, while there is none to deliver. O LORD my God, if I have done this, if there is injustice in my hands, if I have rewarded evil to my friend, or have plundered him who without cause was my adversary, let the enemy pursue my soul and overtake it; and let him trample my life down to the ground and lay my glory in the dust.

Arise, O Lord, in Your anger; lift up Yourself against the rage of my adversaries, and arouse Yourself for me; You have appointed judgment. Let the assembly of the peoples encompass You, and over them return on high. The Lord judges the peoples; vindicate me, O Lord, according to my righteousness and my integrity that is in me. let the evil of the wicked come to an end, but establish the righteous; for the righteous God tries the hearts and minds. My shield is with God, who saves the upright in heart. God is a righteous judge, and a God who has indignation every day. If a man does not repent, He will sharpen His sword; He has bent His bow and made it ready. He has also prepared for Himself deadly weapons; He makes His arrows fiery shafts. Behold, he travails with wickedness, and he conceives mischief and brings forth falsehood. He has dug a pit and hollowed it out, and has fallen into the hole which he made. His mischief will return upon his own head, and his violence will descend upon his own pate. I will give thanks to the Lord according to His righteousness and will sing praise to the name of the Lord Most High.

(Psalm 7 NASB)

OTHER INTERCESSORY PRAYERS IN THE BIBLE:

O Lord, look down from heaven and see us from your holy, glorious home; where is the love for us you used to show—your power, your mercy, and your compassion? Where are they now? Surely you are still our Father! Even if Abraham and Jacob would disown us, still you would be our Father, our Redeemer from ages past. O Lord, why have you hardened our hearts and made us sin and turn against you? Return and help us, for we who belong to you need you so. How briefly we possessed Jerusalem! And now our enemies have destroyed her. O God, why do you treat us as though we weren't your people, as though we were a heathen nation that never called you "Lord"? (Isaiah 63:15–19 TLB)

Oh, that You would rend the heavens! That You would come down! That the mountains might shake at Your presence—as fire burns brushwood, as fire causes water to boil—to make Your name known to Your adversaries, that the nations may tremble at Your presence! When You did awesome things for which we did not look, You came down, the mountains shook at Your presence. For since the beginning of the world men have not heard nor perceived by the ear, nor has the eye seen any God besides You, who acts for the one who waits for Him. You meet him who rejoices and does righteousness, who remembers You in Your ways. You are indeed angry, for we have sinned—in these ways we continue; and we need to be saved. But we are all like an unclean thing, and all our righteousnesses are like filthy rags; we all fade as a leaf, and our iniquities, like the wind, have taken us away. And there is no one who calls on Your name, who stirs himself up to take hold of You; for You have hidden Your face from us, and have consumed us because of our iniquities. But now, O LORD, You are our Father; we are the clay, and You our potter; and all we are the work of Your hand. Do not be furious, O LORD, nor remember iniquity forever; indeed, please look—we all are Your people! (Isaiah 64:1–9)

O my God, I am too ashamed and humiliated to lift up my face to You, my God; for our iniquities have risen higher than our heads, and our guilt has grown up to the heavens. Since the days of our fathers to this day we have been very guilty, and for our iniquities we, our kings, and our priests have been delivered into the hand of the kings of the lands, to the sword, to captivity, to plunder, and to humiliation, as it is this day. And now for a little while grace has been shown from the LORD our God, to leave us a remnant to escape, and to give us a peg in His holy place, that our God may enlighten our eyes and give us a measure of revival in our bondage. For we were slaves. Yet our God did not forsake us in our bondage; but He extended mercy to us.… And now, O our God, what shall we say after this? For we have forsaken Your commandments, which You commanded by Your servants the prophets, saying, "The land which you are entering to possess is an unclean land, with the uncleanness of the peoples of the lands, with their abominations which have filled it from one end to another with their impurity.".… And after all that has come upon us for our evil deeds and for our great guilt, since You our God have punished us less than our iniquities deserve, and have given us such deliverance as this, should we again break Your commandments, and join in marriage with the people committing these abominations? Would You not be angry with us until You had consumed us, so that there would be no remnant or survivor? O LORD God of Israel, You are righteous, for we are left as a remnant, as it is this day. Here we are before You, in our guilt, though no one can stand before You because of this! (Ezra 9:6–11, 13–15)

O LORD, great and awesome God, who keeps His covenant and mercy with those who love Him, and with those who keep His commandments, we have sinned and committed iniquity, we have done wickedly and rebelled, even by departing from Your precepts and Your judgments. Neither have we heeded Your servants the prophets, who spoke in Your name to our kings and our princes, to our fathers and all the people of the land. O LORD, righteousness belongs to You, but to us shame of face…because we have sinned against You. To the LORD our God belong mercy and forgiveness, though we have rebelled against Him. We have not obeyed the voice of the LORD our God, to walk in His laws, which He set before us by His servants the prophets. Yes, all Israel has transgressed

Your law, and has departed so as not to obey Your voice; therefore the curse and the oath written in the Law of Moses the servant of God have been poured out on us, because we have sinned against Him.... O LORD, according to all Your righteousness, I pray, let Your anger and Your fury be turned away from Your city Jerusalem, Your holy mountain; because for our sins, and for the iniquities of our fathers, Jerusalem and Your people are a reproach to all those around us. Now therefore, our God, hear the prayer of Your servant, and his supplications, and for the LORD's sake cause Your face to shine on Your sanctuary, which is desolate. O my God, incline Your ear and hear; open Your eyes and see our desolations, and the city which is called by Your name; for we do not present our supplications before You because of our righteous deeds, but because of Your great mercies. O LORD, hear! O LORD, forgive! O LORD, listen and act! Do not delay for Your own sake, my God, for Your city and Your people are called by Your name.

(Daniel 9:4–11, 16–19)

PRAYERS IN THE PSALMS

You can pray in the actual words of psalms (as demonstrated in the previous prayer resource section, "Scriptural Prayers and Blessings"). For starters, read Psalms 5–10 in your favorite Bible version and ask God to make them special to you.

(Note: in our modern context, the word "enemy" in the Psalms can refer to the power of sin, sickness, and Satan in the church. The word "nations" can refer to the unbelievers in society. "Anger," "wrath," and "judgment" can refer to God's withholding of the fullness of grace toward the church or His anger against an ungodly city or nation.)

This prayer resource, along with the other two in this book, was inspired during the years when I was on staff with Mike Bickle at the Grace Training Center (which preceded the International House of Prayer) in Kansas City.

PSALMS TO PRAY FOR THE OUTPOURING OF THE HOLY SPIRIT:

+ Psalm 44
+ Psalm 45:3–5
+ Psalm 65
+ Psalm 67
+ Psalm 80

Lord, you have poured out amazing blessings on this land! You have restored the fortunes of Israel, and forgiven the sins of your people—yes, covered over each one, so that all your wrath, your blazing anger, is now ended. Now bring us back to loving you, O Lord, so that your anger will never need rise against us again. (Or will you be always angry—on and on to distant generations?) Oh, revive us! Then your people can rejoice in you again. Pour out your love and kindness on us, Lord, and grant us your salvation. I am listening carefully to all the Lord is saying—for he speaks peace to his people, his saints, if they will only stop their sinning. Surely his salvation is near to those who reverence him; our land will be filled with his glory. Mercy and truth have met together. Grim justice and peace have kissed! Truth rises from the earth, and righteousness smiles down from heaven. Yes, the Lord pours down his blessings on the land, and it yields its bountiful crops. Justice goes before him to make a pathway for his steps. (Psalm 85 TLB)

Return, O LORD! How long? And have compassion on Your servants. Oh, satisfy us early with Your mercy, that we may rejoice and be glad all our days! Make us glad according to the days in which You have afflicted us, the years in which we have seen evil. Let Your work appear to Your servants, and Your glory to their children. And let the beauty of the LORD our God be upon us, and establish the work of our hands for us; yes, establish the work of our hands. (Psalm 90:13–17)

Where can I go from your Spirit? Where can I flee from your presence? If I go up to the heavens, you are there; if I make my bed in the depths, you are there. If I rise on the wings of the dawn, if I settle on the far side of the sea, even there your hand will guide me, your right hand will hold me fast. If I say, "Surely the darkness will hide me and the light become night around me," even the darkness will not be dark to you; the night will shine like the day, for darkness is as light to you. For you created my inmost being; you knit me together in my mother's womb. I praise you because I am fearfully and wonderfully made; your works are wonderful, I know that full well. My frame was not hidden from you when I was made in the secret place, when I was woven together in the depths of the earth. Your eyes saw my unformed body; all the days ordained for me were written in your book before one of them came to be. How precious to me are your thoughts, God! How vast is the sum of them! Were I to count them, they would outnumber the grains of sand—when I awake, I am still with you.

(Psalm 139:7–18 NIV)

PSALMS TO PRAY IN TIMES OF PERSONAL DEFEAT OR NEED FOR HELP:

- Psalm 6
- Psalm 13
- Psalm 25
- Psalm 41
- Psalm 43
- Psalm 69
- Psalm 83
- Psalm 86
- Psalm 88
- Psalm 137

Have mercy on me, O God, according to your unfailing love; according to your great compassion blot out my transgressions. Wash away all my iniquity and cleanse me from my sin. For I know my transgressions, and my sin is always before me. Against you, you only, have I sinned and done what is evil in your sight; so you are right in your verdict and justified when you judge. Surely I was sinful at birth, sinful from the time my mother conceived me. Yet you desired faithfulness even in the womb; you taught me wisdom in that secret place. Cleanse me with hyssop, and I will be clean; wash me, and I will be whiter than snow. Let me hear joy and gladness; let the bones you have crushed rejoice. Hide your face from my sins and blot out all my iniquity. Create in me a pure heart, O God, and renew a steadfast spirit within me. Do not cast me from your presence or take your Holy Spirit from me. Restore to me the joy of your salvation and grant me a willing spirit, to sustain me. Then I will teach transgressors your ways, so that sinners will turn back to you. Deliver me from the guilt of bloodshed, O God, you who are God my Savior, and my tongue will sing of your righteousness. Open my lips, Lord, and my mouth will declare your praise. You do not delight in sacrifice, or I would bring it; you do not take pleasure in burnt offerings. My sacrifice, O God, is a broken spirit; a broken and contrite heart you, God, will not despise. (Psalm 51:1–17 NIV)

Out of the depths I cry to you, LORD; Lord, hear my voice. Let your ears be attentive to my cry for mercy. If you, LORD, kept a record of sins, Lord, who could stand? But with you there is forgiveness, so that we can, with reverence, serve you. I wait for the LORD, my whole being waits, and in his word I put my hope. I wait for the Lord more than watchmen wait for the morning, more than watchmen wait for the morning. Israel, put your hope in the LORD, for with the LORD is unfailing love and with him is full redemption. He himself will redeem Israel from all their sins. (Psalm 130 NIV)

_____

_____

_____

_____

_____

_____

PSALMS OF PERSONAL DEVOTION:

- Psalm 25
- Psalm 26
- Psalm 40
- Psalm 42
- Psalm 45
- Psalm 63
- Psalm 65
- Psalm 84
- Psalm 86
- Psalm 102:12–22
- Psalm 110:1–5

The LORD is my light and my salvation; whom shall I fear? The LORD is the strength of my life; of whom shall I be afraid? When the wicked came against me to eat up my flesh, my enemies and foes, they stumbled and fell. Though an army may encamp against me, my heart shall not fear; though war may rise against me, in this I will be confident. One thing I have desired of the LORD, that will I seek: that I may dwell in the house of the LORD all the days of my life, to behold the beauty of the LORD, and to inquire in His temple. For in the time of trouble He shall hide me in His pavilion; in the secret place of His tabernacle He shall hide me; He shall set me high upon a rock. And now my head shall be lifted up above my enemies all around me; therefore I will offer sacrifices of joy in His tabernacle; I will sing, yes, I will sing praises to the LORD. Hear, O LORD, when I cry with my voice! Have mercy also upon me, and answer me. When You said, "Seek My face," my heart said to You, "Your face, LORD, I will seek." Do not hide Your face from me; do not turn Your servant away in anger; You have been my help; do not leave me nor forsake me, O God of my salvation. When my father and my mother forsake me, then the LORD will take care of me. Teach me Your way, O LORD, and lead me in a smooth path, because of my enemies. Do not deliver me to the will of my adversaries; for false witnesses have risen against me, and such as breathe out violence. I would have lost heart, unless I had believed that I would see the goodness of the LORD in the land of the living. Wait on the LORD; be of good courage, and He shall strengthen your heart; wait, I say, on the LORD!   (Psalm 27)

I will give You thanks with all my heart; I will sing praises to You before the gods. I will bow down toward Your holy temple and give thanks to Your name for Your lovingkindness and Your truth; for You have magnified Your word according to all Your name. On the day I called, You answered me; You made me bold with strength in my soul. All the kings of the earth will give thanks to You, O LORD, when they have heard the words of Your mouth. And they will sing of the ways of the LORD, for great is the glory of the LORD. For though the LORD is exalted, yet He regards the lowly, but the haughty He knows from afar. Though I walk in the midst of trouble, You will revive me; You will stretch forth Your hand against the wrath of my enemies, and Your right hand will save me. The LORD will accomplish what concerns me; Your lovingkindness, O LORD, is everlasting; do not forsake the works of Your hands.   (Psalm 138 NASB)

PROPHETIC PROMISES OF RESTORATION

Acts 3:21 tells us that Jesus will not come again until the period of the church's restoration, which was promised by the holy prophets. What, exactly, are these promises spoken by the holy prophets?

The following Scriptures are promises of restoration or revival from all sixteen of the prophets, from Isaiah to Malachi. These promises are to be fulfilled by both physical and spiritual Israel. (See Romans 4:1–17; 9:6–8; Galatians 3:28–29; Hebrews 12:22–23.)

Like the previous two appendices, "Prophetic Promises of Restoration" was inspired during the years when I was on staff with Mike Bickle at the Grace Training Center (which preceded the International House of Prayer) in Kansas City.

PROMISES FROM ISAIAH:

1. Isaiah 4:2–6: God will purify His people, and Jesus will be glorious in the church.

2. Isaiah 5:16: God will remove sin and demonstrate His power.

3. Isaiah 27:6: Revival will cover the earth "in that day" (in the end times).

4. Isaiah 28:5: God's reigning power will be demonstrated.

5. Isaiah 29:14, 17–24: Revival includes signs and wonders with many children (new converts).

6. Isaiah 30:18–26: God desires and wants to give grace; when prayer is offered, revival will come.

7. Isaiah 32:12–20: Pray and mourn until revival comes.

8. Isaiah 33:13–14: The conviction of the Word will greatly increase.

9. Isaiah 33:21–24: Healing for all will come like a river.

10. Isaiah 34:16–17: God declares it will happen according to His Word.

11. Isaiah 35:1–10: Revival will come with power, with miracles, and with grace to make the church holy.

12. Isaiah 37:14–20: An example of prayer for deliverance from opposition (equating the Assyrians with the devil).

13. Isaiah 40:30–31: God will anoint people who pray; wait for God.

14. Isaiah 41:8–20: God has chosen us to destroy the devil and to bring rivers of anointing to the afflicted.

15. Isaiah 42:6–9: We will see healing, and a "new thing" will spring forth.

16. Isaiah 42:18–21: This new move of God will come with rivers of anointing.

17. Isaiah 43:5–7: Worldwide revival will include protection from evil.

18. Isaiah 44:1–6: The rivers of anointing will flow on a thirsty church.

19. Isaiah 45:8: God intercedes for the church and the nation of Israel.

20. Isaiah 45:22–25: God will raise up Jesus's name and save many souls.

21. Isaiah 46:8–11: God will do it.

22. Isaiah 46:13: God's glory and salvation will come to physical and spiritual Israel.

23. Isaiah 49:4: God will show justice on behalf of Jesus's death and resurrection.

24. Isaiah 49:6: Jesus's light and salvation through the church will cover the earth.

25. Isaiah 49:7–13: Kings will bow to Jesus as His people restore the land by the Spirit.

26. Isaiah 49:14–26: God will not forget us. There will be many new converts, and our enemy will be defeated.

27. Isaiah 51:3–6: God's power will be demonstrated.

28. Isaiah 51:9–11: Isaiah is telling God to awake and to do now what He did through Moses.

29. Isaiah 51:14–16: Those in sin and sickness will be delivered by the anointing on the church.

30. Isaiah 52:13–15: Jesus's name will be exalted in this city.

31. Isaiah 53:10–12: Jesus's church will prosper and divide the spoil.

32. Isaiah 54:3–17: Revival will come, through God's sure love.

33. Isaiah 58:8–12: God's light and glory will shine in revival if we give to the poor.

34. Isaiah 59:19–21: God will be as a mighty, rushing stream through us.

35. Isaiah 60:1; 62:12: A picture of revival. (Find specific verses to believe for.)

36. Isaiah 61:7: You will inherit a double portion.

37. Isaiah 63:7–14: Isaiah recounts God's glorious deeds as seen in Exodus through Moses. For us, this promise can refer to the deeds performed by Peter and Paul in the book of Acts.

38. Isaiah 63:15; 64:12: Isaiah leads in intercessory prayer for revival.

39. Isaiah 65:1–7: God answers Isaiah 64:12 with, "No, I will not restrain or withhold Myself from praying people since I answered those who did not even seek Me."

_____

_____

_____

_____

_____

PROMISES AND PRAYERS FROM JEREMIAH (BOOK OF JEREMIAH):

1. Jeremiah 1:12: God will watch over His Word (promises of restoration) to perform it.

2. Jeremiah's intercessory burdens:
   - Jeremiah 8:18
   - Jeremiah 10:19
   - Jeremiah 13:17
   - Jeremiah 14:17
   - Jeremiah 23:9

3. Jeremiah 14:7–9; 19:22: Intercessory prayer for revival.

4. Jeremiah 7:12–18: Jeremiah's personal worship and prayer.

5. Jeremiah 23:29: God's Word under the anointing is like a fire and a hammer.

6. Jeremiah 24:6–7: For revival.

7. Jeremiah 29:10–14: Revival will come through prayer.

8. Jeremiah 30:3, 9–11, 16–22: Sin will be conquered and blessing will flow.

9. Jeremiah 30:24: God's wisdom will be released in the end times.

10. Jeremiah 31:1–14, 17, 20–26, 31–40: Revival promises for physical and spiritual Israel.

11. Jeremiah 32:17–25: Jeremiah's intercessory prayer for revival.

12. Jeremiah 33:3: Prayer is the key to revival.

13. Jeremiah 33:6–26: Blessing and power will come when God restores His people.

14. Jeremiah 50:4–7, 17–20, 33–34: Promise of being forgiven and restored to the level of the believers in the book of Acts.

15. Jeremiah 51:20–23: God will make us His weapon.

_____

_____

_____

_____

_____

_____

PROMISES FROM JEREMIAH (BOOK OF LAMENTATIONS):

In the book of Lamentations, the church (Zion) without revival mourns for the fullness of God. The mourning is for more power and grace. "The enemy" is a picture of the devil. The key passage is Lamentations 2:18–20.

PRAYERS IN LAMENTATIONS:

+ Lamentations 1:9, 11, 16
+ Lamentations 2:12–13
+ Lamentations 2:18–20
+ Lamentations 3:20–26
+ Lamentations 3:31–33
+ Lamentations 5:1–22

_____

_____

_____

_____

_____

_____

PROMISES FROM EZEKIEL:

1. Ezekiel 11:14–21: God will gather and redeem from the whole world.

2. Ezekiel 16:60–63: God will restore and never again will we backslide into shame.

3. Ezekiel 33:1–9: The prophet's responsibility is to say what God says even if opposition comes.

4. Ezekiel 34:11–16: Promise of both physical and spiritual revival.

5. Ezekiel 34:25–31: Promise of restoration.

6. Ezekiel 36:8–15: Promises of new converts and success over enemies in the Holy Spirit.

7. Ezekiel 36:22–32: God will exalt Jesus's name in our sight.

8. Ezekiel 36:33–38: The heathen will see God's blessings on us.

9. Ezekiel 37:24–28: God's covenant and blessings will be manifested in unity and power.

10. Ezekiel 39:25–29: We will know God is in our midst in power.

11. Ezekiel 47:1–9: Rivers from the heavenly temple will flow.

_____

_____

_____

_____

_____

_____

PROMISES AND PRAYERS FROM DANIEL:

1. Daniel 7:18–27: Believers will prevail over the devil through God's grace.

2. Daniel 9:9–19: The prayer of Daniel, the premiere intercessor, that released Israel from captivity into revival.

_____

_____

_____

_____

_____

_____

PROMISES FROM HOSEA:

1. Hosea 1:7, 10: Grace will deliver us and we will be called "sons of the living God."

2. Hosea 2:19–23: Once we are joined intimately to God's grace, refreshment will flow from heaven.

3. Hosea 3:5: The Jews will be saved in the end-time revival.

4. Hosea 5:15; 6:3: God will not withhold but will come as the rain.

5. Hosea 6:11: God will fully restore the church.

6. Hosea 10:12: Righteousness will rain on our hearts.

7. Hosea 11:1, 3–4, 8–11; 12:10: Remind God of these facts.

8. Hosea 14:4–7: God will heal freely and His church will blossom.

_____

_____

_____

_____

_____

_____

PROMISES FROM JOEL:

1. Joel 2:17: Intercessory prayer will be answered.

2. Joel 2:18–20: God will be zealous.

3. Joel 2:23–29: A worldwide revival of power is coming.

4. Joel 3:1: God will restore the fortunes of His people.

5. Joel 3:17–20: The church will be holy and established by God.

_____

_____

_____

_____

_____

_____

PROMISES FROM AMOS:

Amos 9:11–15: God will rebuild the tabernacle of David and restore worship in the Spirit.

_____

_____

_____

_____

_____

_____

PROMISES FROM OBADIAH:

Obadiah 1:17–21: The church will experience power and will prevail against all sin (Esau).

_____

_____

_____

_____

_____

_____

PROMISES AND PRAYERS FROM MICAH:

1. Micah 2:12: Israel and the church will be restored.

2. Micah 4:12–13: God will thresh the harvest through the church.

3. Micah 5:3–4: God will return to His people in power to shepherd them.

4. Micah 5:7–9: Blessings from heaven will fall.

5. Micah 7:7–20: Micah's intercessory prayer for revival.

_____

_____

_____

_____

_____

PROMISES AND PRAYERS FROM HABAKKUK:

1. Habakkuk 2:14: The earth will be filled with God's glory and worldwide revival.

2. Habakkuk 3:2: Habakkuk's intercessory prayer.

_____

_____

_____

_____

_____

_____

PROMISES FROM ZEPHANIAH:

1. Zephaniah 3:9: Holiness and unity will come.

2. Zephaniah 3:12–20: The church will be purified and prosperous.

_____

_____

_____

_____

_____

_____

PROMISES FROM HAGGAI:

Haggai 2:4, 9: God will be with us to make His end-time church more glorious than the first-century church.

_____

_____

_____

_____

_____

_____

PROMISES FROM ZECHARIAH:

1. Zechariah 1:3: God will return to His people with power and grace.

2. Zechariah 1:12–17: God will reward the people appropriately.

3. Zechariah 2:4–5: Glory will protect the church.

4. Zechariah 2:9–13: Revival, through God being in our midst.

5. Zechariah 6:12–15: Jesus will build His church with great authority.

6. Zechariah 8:2–3: God will be jealous for revival in the church.

7. Zechariah 8:7–13: God will treat His people with favor.

8. Zechariah 8:20–23: Promise of worldwide revival.

9. Zechariah 9:11–17: A picture of revival.

10. Zechariah 10:1: Promise of rain (anointing) in response to prayer.

11. Zechariah 10:3–5: The believers will be mighty in God.

12. Zechariah 10:6–9: For revival.

13. Zechariah 10:12: Promise for strength by grace.

14. Zechariah 12:3–11: Revival fire and power; the Spirit of grace and prayer.

15. Zechariah 13:1–4, 9: Revival.

16. Zechariah 14:9: God's name alone will be exalted on earth.

_____

_____

_____

_____

_____

_____

PROMISES FROM MALACHI:

1. Malachi 1:11: Jesus's name will be great in all the earth.

2. Malachi 3:1: Jesus will suddenly visit His people.

3. Malachi 3:7, 10–12: Jesus will supply until there is no more need.

4. Malachi 4:2–3: Jesus will be exalted by healings.

5. Malachi 4:5–6: Elijah is coming with great power.

_____

_____

_____

_____

_____

BIBLIOGRAPHY AND FURTHER RECOMMENDED READINGS

Alves, Elizabeth. *Becoming a Prayer Warrior*. Grand Rapids, MI: Chosen Books, 2016.

Alves, Elizabeth, Tommi Femrite, and Karen Kaufman. *Intercessors: Discover Your Prayer Power*. Grand Rapids, MI: Chosen Books, 2000.

The Book of Common Prayer. New York: Church Hymnal Corporation, 1943.

Bounds, E. M. *The Necessity of Prayer*. New Kensington, PA: Whitaker House, 1984.

Campbell, Ron G. *Free from Freemasonry*. Grand Rapids, MI: Baker Publishing Group, 1999.

Crist, Terry. *Interceding Against the Powers of Darkness*. Tulsa, OK: Terry Crist Ministries, 1990.

Dawson, John. *Taking Our Cities for God*. Lake Mary, FL: Charisma House, 1989, 2001.

———. *Healing America's Wounds*. Grand Rapids, MI: Baker Publishing Group, 1994.

Easton, M. [Matthew] G. [George], M.A., D.D., "Scourging," *Illustrated Bible Dictionary*. 3rd. ed. New York: T. Nelson and Sons, 1897.

Frangipane, Francis. *The House of the Lord.* Lake Mary, FL: Charisma House, 1996.

Goll, James W. *The Coming Israel Awakening.* Grand Rapids, MI: Chosen Books, 2009.

———. *Deliverance from Darkness.* Grand Rapids, MI: Chosen Books, 2010.

———. *The Discerner.* New Kensington, PA: Whitaker House, 2017.

———. *Intercession: The Power and Passion to Shape History.* Shippensburg, PA: Destiny Image, 2011.

———. *The Lifestyle of a Watchman.* Grand Rapids, MI: Chosen Books, 2017.

———. *The Lost Art of Intercession.* Rev. and exp. ed. Shippensburg, PA: Destiny Image, 2016.

———. *The Lost Art of Practicing His Presence.* Shippensburg, PA: Destiny Image, 2007.

———. *Passionate Pursuit.* New Kensington, PA: Whitaker House, 2015.

———. *Prayer Storm.* Shippensburg, PA: Destiny Image, 2013.

———. *Prayer Storm Study Guide: The Hour That Changes the World.* Shippensburg, PA: Destiny Image, 2008.

———. *Praying for Israel's Destiny.* Grand Rapids, MI: Chosen Books, 2005.

———. *Praying with God's Heart: The Power and Purpose of Prophetic Intercession.* Grand Rapids, MI: Chosen Books, 2018. (Formerly titled *The Prophetic Intercessor.*)

———. *Releasing Spiritual Gifts Today.* New Kensington, PA: Whitaker House, 2016.

Goll, James W., and Chris DuPré. *The Lost Art of Pure Worship.* Shippensburg, PA: Destiny Image, 2012.

Goll, James W., and Lou Engel, *The Call of the Elijah Revolution.* Shippensburg, PA: Destiny Image, 2008.

Grubb, Norman. *Rees Howells, Intercessor.* Fort Washington, PA: CLC Publications, 2016.

Hawthorne, Steve, and Graham Kendrick. *Prayerwalking: Praying On-Site with Insight.* Lake Mary, FL: Charisma House, 1993.

Jacobs, Cindy. "Dealing with Strongholds." In *Breaking Spiritual Strongholds in Your City,* edited by C. Peter Wagner, 73–93. Shippensburg, PA: Destiny Image, 2015.

———. *Deliver Us from Evil.* Ventura, CA: Regal Books, 2001.

Matrisciana, Caryl. *Gods of the New Age.* Irvine, CA: Harvest House, 1985.

McLaughlin, Pamela. *Chosen Treasures.* Self-published, 2013.

Murray, Andrew. *With Christ in the School of Prayer.* New Kensington, PA: Whitaker House, 1981.

Otis Jr., George. "An Overview of Spiritual Mapping." In *Breaking Spiritual Strongholds in Your City,* edited by C. Peter Wagner, 33–50. Shippensburg, PA: Destiny Image, 2015.

Prince, Derek. *Blessing or Curse: You Can Choose.* Grand Rapids, MI: Chosen Books, 2008.

———. *Prayers and Proclamations.* New Kensington, PA: Whitaker House, 2010.

———. *Pulling Down Strongholds.* New Kensington, PA: Whitaker House, 2013.

Sherman, Dean. *Spiritual Warfare for Every Christian.* Seattle, WA: YWAM Publishing, 1990.

Silvoso, Ed. *That None Should Perish.* Ventura, CA: Regal Books, 1994.

Wagner, C. Peter. *Warfare Prayer.* Shippensburg, PA: Destiny Image, 1992, 2001, rev. 2009.

ABOUT THE AUTHOR

James W. Goll is the founder of God Encounters Ministries. He is also the founder of Prayer Storm and the Worship City Alliance, as well as the cofounder of Women on the Frontlines and Compassion Acts. James is a member of the Harvest International Ministries Apostolic Team and the Apostolic Council of Prophetic Elders. He serves as a core instructor in the Wagner Leadership Institute.

After pastoring in the Midwest United States, James was thrust into the role of an international equipper and trainer. He has traveled to over fifty nations, carrying a passion for Jesus wherever he goes. His desire is to see the body of Christ become the house of prayer for all nations and be empowered by the Holy Spirit to spread the good news of Jesus to every country and to all peoples.

James and Michal Ann Goll were married for thirty-two years before her graduation to heaven in the fall of 2008. James has four married children and a growing number of grandchildren. He makes his home in Franklin, Tennessee.

For more information:

James W. Goll
God Encounters Ministries
P.O. Box 1653 ✦ Franklin, TN 37065
Phone: 1-877-200-1604

Website:
www.godencounters.com

E-mails:
info@godencounters.com
cs@godencounters.com ✦ classes@godencounters.com

Social Media:
Facebook, Instagram, Twitter, GEM Media, XP Media,
Kingdom Flame, YouTube, Vimeo, Charisma blogs, iTunes podcasts

ADDITIONAL MATERIALS BY JAMES W. GOLL

(Many titles feature a matching study guide as well as audio and video presentations.)

Adventures in the Prophetic (with Michal Ann Goll, Mickey Robinson, Patricia King, Jeff Jansen, and Ryan Wyatt)

Angelic Encounters (with Michal Ann Goll)

The Call to the Elijah Revolution (with Lou Engle)

The Coming Israel Awakening

Deliverance from Darkness

The Discerner

Dream Language (with Michal Ann Goll)

Exploring Your Dreams and Visions

Finding Hope

God Encounters Today (with Michal Ann Goll)

Hearing God's Voice Today

The Lost Art of Intercession

The Lost Art of Practicing His Presence

The Lost Art of Pure Worship (with Chris Dupré and contributions from Jeff Deyo, Sean Feucht, Julie Meyer, and Rachel Goll Tucker)

The Lifestyle of a Prophet

The Lifestyle of a Watchman

Living a Supernatural Life

Passionate Pursuit

Prayer Storm

Praying for Israel's Destiny

Praying with God's Heart

A Radical Faith

Releasing Spiritual Gifts Today

The Seer

Shifting Shadows of Supernatural Experiences (with Julia Loren)

Women on the Frontlines series: *A Call to Compassion, A Call to Courage,* and *A Call to the Secret Place* (Michal Ann Goll with James W. Goll)

Free Inspiring Messages

| ▶ Video | 🎧 Audio | 📶 Blog |

Did you know that we have hundreds of free teaching articles, as well as audio and video messages for you to stream or download?

We believe they will revitalize you and give you hope.

It's amazing how far a little inspiration, encouragement and even challenge can go to help you break through old ruts and places of stagnancy in your spiritual life.

Stir up the fire in your spiritual life today!

GOD ENCOUNTERS MINISTRIES
with James W. Goll

Go to
www.GodEncounters.com

Welcome to Our House!

We Have a Special Gift for You

It is our privilege and pleasure to share in your love of Christian books. We are committed to bringing you authors and books that feed, challenge, and enrich your faith.

To show our appreciation, we invite you to sign up to receive a specially selected **Reader Appreciation Gift**, with our compliments. Just go to the Web address at the bottom of this page.

God bless you as you seek a deeper walk with Him!

WE HAVE A GIFT FOR YOU. VISIT:

whpub.me/nonfictionthx

WHITAKER
HOUSE